IN PRAISE OF
NOT JUST A SURVIVOR...

I have just turned the last page of 'your mom's memoirs'. I am in total awe of a woman I never knew & feel so grateful to be given insight into & to share in her life. It is, by far, the most compelling account of an horrendous period in time & a poignant dedication of a daughter to her mother, that I have ever read.

Denise Shulman, *Brisbane, Australia*

I started reading your Mum's biography and I just could not stop. Thanks to your powerful writing, I feel that I know her, her family, what she went through at that horrific time and what motivated her to ensure that her experiences would be shared to make certain that the Holocaust would never be forgotten. Placing your mother's words so strategically throughout added so much veracity and authenticity to the story.

Philip Zavelsky, *former owner American Book Store, Brisbane, Australia*

This is a beautiful tribute to a strong, formidable woman who survived against all odds.

Mandy Herbert, *Freelance Editor, Melbourne, Australia*

And now that I have started reading, I cannot put it down... you have created the space for her to live and breathe in your words. **Gill Fine**, *Australia*

I actually found myself thinking about this book for weeks after I finished reading it. The many voices in the book were a perfect vehicle to express how important Bobba was to her family, and how her experiences during the Holocaust informed and influenced not only all aspects of her life, but the lives of her family members as well. I have read many books about the Holocaust and those who survived it and I really feel that this is a unique work. To have Bobba's actual words from her recordings, added a deep and personal dimension to the book.

Pam Weisbrod, *Florida, USA*

NOT JUST A SURVIVOR

a portrait of my mother

Rochy Miller

Copyright © 2020 Rae Miller

All rights reserved. No part of this book may be used or reproduced by any means, graphic, electronic, or mechanical. Including photocopying, recording, taping or by any information storage retrieval system without the written permission of the author, except in the case of brief quotations embodied in critical articles and reviews.

ISBN 978-0-9942286-8-0

*This book is dedicated to the memory of
two special women –*

my Mother and my Sister.

I am eternally grateful to you both for the life we shared.

Rochy Miller, (author), Lea Leibowitz (my mother),
Sheila Uliel, (my sister) 1988

THANKS

Writing this book has been an emotional journey – one I have undertaken with lots of support from my family and friends.

Thank you to so many people:

To my husband – for supporting me through the initial emotional traumas of listening to my mother's words on tape, night after night, recounting her harrowing experiences; for reading the manuscript – again and again as it kept evolving; and for always believing in my ability to tell this story in the way it needed to be told.

To my daughter, Kerry – who, alongside all the practical help in formatting the early drafts and designing the cover – was always there to discuss the words, the ideas, the stories, the concepts, and the hurdles; and who kept nudging and gently pushing to make sure I reached the goalposts – whatever it took.

To my son, David – for all the technical support – helping to get the words from one format to another and keeping me sane when the computer technology became my nemesis!

To Eytan – who did such an incredible job of editing the book – sharing his talent and insight, reading and re-reading and honing my drafts into a polished book in which we both share an emotional investment.

To my amazing friends, and editors, who read, edited, commented, suggested, applauded and generally made me believe in the merits of this book – thank you on so many levels.

And finally, to my mother – whose remarkable life and awe-inspiring character, made this story possible. I hope I've done you proud!

CONTENTS

INTRODUCTION 15
THE TIMELINE 21
THE FAMILY TREE 24

PART ONE: FAMILY   27

    Chapter 1. HER PARENTS 29
    Chapter 2. MOKKA 41
    Chapter 3. MICHAEL 55
    Chapter 4. HYMIE 59
    Chapter 5. SAMUEL 67
    Chapter 6. THE EXTENDED FAMILY 81
    Chapter 7. THE GRANDCHILDREN 93

PART TWO: FRIENDSHIP   101

    Chapter 8. EARLY FRIENDSHIPS 103
    Chapter 9. FRIENDS IN THE CAMPS 107
    Chapter 10. FRIENDS AND LIBERATION 119
    Chapter 11. FRIENDS IN A NEW WORLD 127

PART THREE: FOOD   137

    Chapter 12. MY MOTHER AND FOOD 139
    Chapter 13. FOOD IN THE GHETTO 149

Chapter 14. FOOD IN THE CAMPS 155

Chapter 15. FOOD AFTER LIBERATION 177

PART FOUR: EDUCATION   181

Chapter 16. EDUCATION IN LITHUANIA 183

Chapter 17. STUDY AS A PRACTICAL SOLUTION 189

Chapter 18. STUDY AS THERAPY 191

PART FIVE: THE HOLOCAUST   203

Chapter 19. SURVIVAL 207

Chapter 20. HOW COULD IT HAPPEN? 217

Chapter 21. RESISTANCE 223

Chapter 22. HER MISSION 229

PART SIX: ZIONISM, JUDAISM AND DEATH   233

Chapter 23. ZIONISM 235

Chapter 24. JUDAISM 241

Chapter 25. DEATH 245

ADDENDUM: REFLECTIONS ON BOBBA   249

INTRODUCTION

My mother, Lea, Kovno, 1935

My mother was a survivor.

Within five minutes of meeting her, whoever you were, and whatever the circumstances of your meeting, she would identify herself as a Holocaust survivor.

It was how she defined herself; it formed the frame of reference that explained everything about her – her belief system, her opinions, her health, her actions.

The Holocaust, and her experience of it, was the central tenet of her life. It was the eternal flame that flickered within her – always burning as a reminder of who she was, and why she was alive. She justified her survival by her mission to educate others. She spoke about the Holocaust to everyone who asked and at every opportunity. She spoke to groups at the Holocaust Museum, to school students, in interviews, to social gatherings – as an academic and in her personal capacity.

My mother embodied the Holocaust. She experienced it physically, lived it emotionally and studied it intellectually.

She spent her entire life trying to make sense of an inexplicable trauma that ruled her present life and had decimated her past. She attended courses at Yad Vashem, went to public lectures, read countless books, watched almost everything screened about the Holocaust, and studied it at university – writing a doctoral thesis on Holocaust Literature when she was almost 70 years old.

My mother passed away in 2000 at the age of 86.

As a consequence of her prolific speaking and writing about the Holocaust, and her willingness to expose the intimacies of her life in the name of education, there are many, many records of her story. There are audio and television interviews, recordings of her lectures, written notes, newspaper articles, and video interviews prepared for the Shoah Series and for Yad Vashem.

I had intended to transcribe these, to document them in a way that would ensure her grandchildren and great-grandchildren would find, in her words and her deeds, the essence of who she was. But as I listened to her recorded voice, I came to realise that relating her Holocaust experience – seminal as it was – was not enough.

INTRODUCTION

Despite her definition of herself in this way, and no matter how dominant this self-image loomed in her psyche, being a Survivor was never all of who she was.

To us, her extended family, and to all the many people whom she touched with her story, she was so much more.

Calling on the many stories told and retold – some by her, and some about her – that fill our collective memories, I am hoping a composite of the warm, intelligent and amazing person that she was, will emerge. Coloured as these memories are, by love, time and the slanted perception of hindsight, I nevertheless hope they will paint a true portrait of her – of not just a Holocaust survivor, but of somebody who was truly remarkable, someone who survived and enriched people's lives not because of the Holocaust, but despite it.

In her absence, her family has grown. A whole new generation has been born who will never experience the profound impact she inevitably had on anyone who met her. And for those of us who did know her – who were privileged to experience her world from her sharing – the sad reality is that the intensity of this knowledge is fading. The details are blurring – transforming from ever-present larger-than-life daily mantras to valuable but infrequently read volumes on the dusty shelves of memory.

It is in the hope of not just preserving these memories, but infusing them with the heart and breath and wisdom of the wonderful, inspiring and unique person that lived them, that these stories are being re-told.

These are her stories.

A note to the reader ...

Many parts of the story are told in my mother's own words.

They appear in this font, indented, between two lines, and are literal transcripts from her interviews, lectures and documents. They have only been minimally modified to aid clarity.

THE TIMELINE

5 July 1914	Lea Charif (my mother) born Byutichik, Lithuania
1936	Graduated Kovno University, Lithuania
22 May 1937	Married Moses Klompus
7 June 1938	Gave birth to son, Michael
22 June 1940	Russia invades Lithuania
22 June 1941	Germany invades Lithuania
26 October 1942	Separated from family
1942 – 1945	First concentration camp: Vaivara, Estonia
	Second concentration camp: Erida, Estonia
	Third Concentration camp: Lagedy, Estonia
	Transfer to Stutthof, Germany
	Fourth Concentration camp: Ochsenzoll Germany
12 March 1945	Fifth Concentration camp: Bergen-Belsen, Germany
15 April 1945	Liberated Bergen-Belsen, Germany
11 July 1946	Arrived South Africa
28 April 1948	Married Samuel Leibowitz (my father)
December 1949	B. A. degree University of Witwatersrand, South Africa
29 January 1950	Sheila (my sister) born
31 March 1954	Rochy (me) born

1963	B. A. Honours degree University of Witwatersrand, South Africa
1966	B. Ed. degree University of Witwatersrand, South Africa
1967	Started P.H.D. degree University of Witwatersrand, South Africa
16 June 1976	Samuel (my father) died
1990	Emigrated to Sydney, Australia
5 August 2000	Lea (my mother) died

NOT JUST A SURVIVOR

THE FAMILY TREE

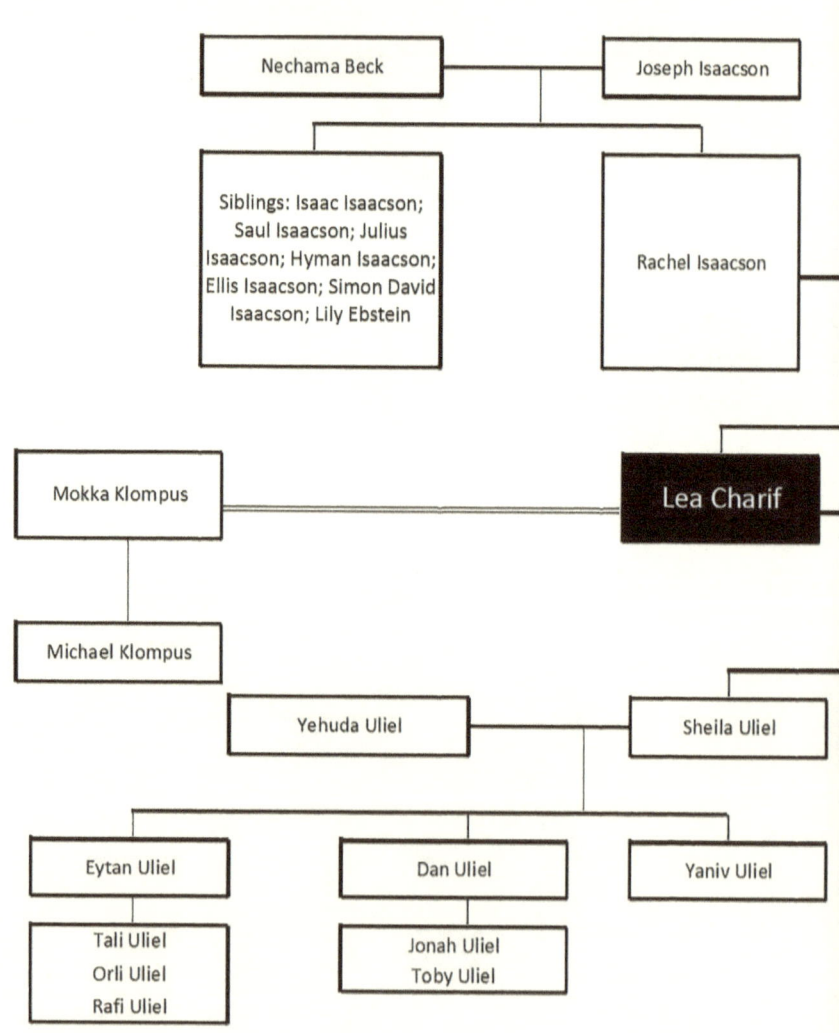

THE FAMILY TREE

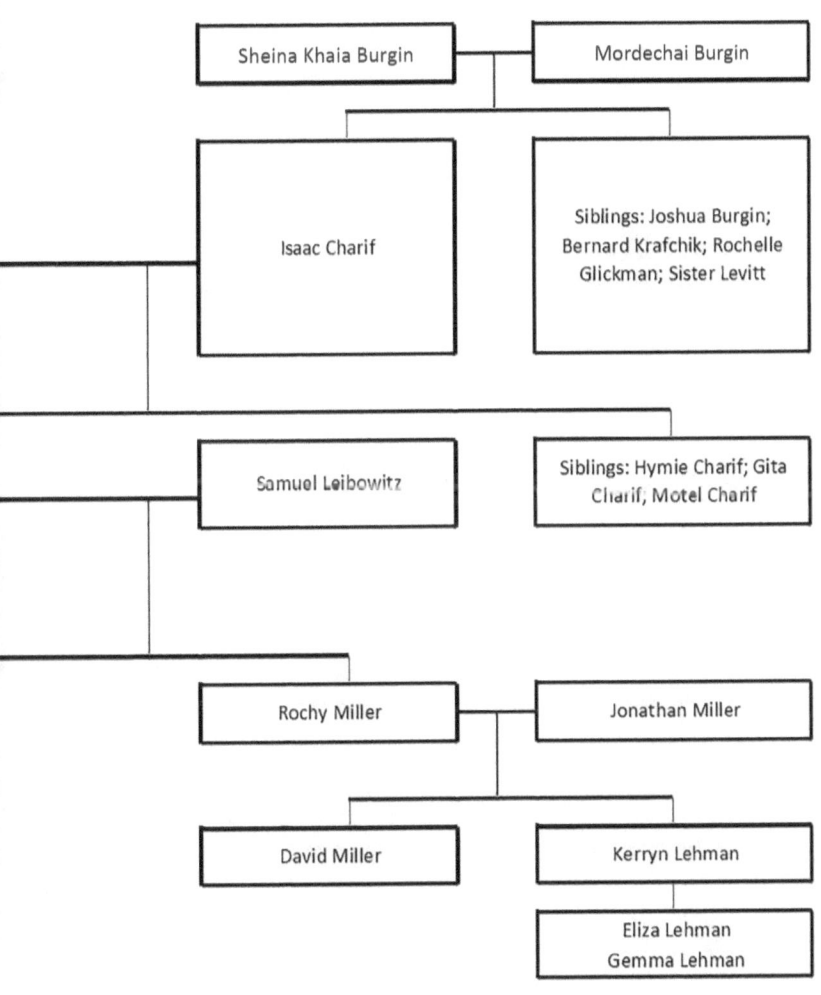

PART ONE:
FAMILY

In her eighty-six years, my mother lived on three continents and had two separate families. But she defined her life in two timeframes: before the Holocaust and after – as if that cataclysmic event had cleaved two separate worlds.

Before the Holocaust, she lived in Lithuania. She had a complete, extended family: grandparents, parents, siblings, a husband and a child. She always spoke of this time and place as 'home'.

After the Holocaust, she lived in South Africa, then Australia. She had fractured remnants of her first family: one remaining sibling, some uncles and aunts and cousins, and some relatives of her first husband. She also had a whole new family: Samuel, her husband, two daughters – Sheila and me – and five grandchildren.

In both lives, family was paramount.

She somehow managed to amalgamate the elements of both, although living between these two juxtaposed worlds was always difficult for her.

The past continually cast shadows on her present.

CHAPTER 1.
HER PARENTS

(LITHUANIA, PRE-1942)

*Isaac and Rachel (my grandparents),
Lea, Gita and Mottel (Lea's young siblings) c.1928*

There is a big house. The adjacent shed is filled with farming implements and winter food – hay and straw and the grains – corn, wheat and barley – that *our father has reaped. In front of the house there is a large vegetable garden, filled with every kind of vegetable to last the family through the summer, and enough to be pickled in big casks for the winter. A stretch of level ground is covered with soft, green grass. Soon our father will cut it with a scythe, dry it and store the hay for the winter. At the side of the garden there is a deep well. Close by, there is a big lake, and our father and neighbours go out regularly in rowing boats, with fishing nets, and share the catch. These healthy and plentiful surroundings provide an idyllic childhood.*

(From a letter by Hymie, my mother's older brother, to his children.)

HER PARENTS

My mother, Lea, was born in Lithuania, in 1914, the second of four children. She had an older brother, Hymie, a younger sister Gita and a younger brother, Mottel.

In all the stories she told of her childhood, her father stood out as the central figure. He was a tall, imposing but loving man, who worked as the groundsman and caretaker of a large rural estate.

My mother always told us the estate was one of the Summer Palaces of Czar Nikolai of Russia, and that she was born during his reign in that palace. She details in many interviews the relationship her parents had with the Russian Royal Family.

> Well, I don't know much about the Russian King, but my parents used to tell me they used to come for a holiday during summer with the princesses, and my oldest brother he was playing with one of the princesses. I don't know who it was. Life was very nice there and the King and the Queen were very nice to my parents. My mother used to bake for them, and cook fish.

My mother had an accurate and vivid memory. She recalled in detail a trip she and her father took back to the estate where she had been born, many years later. She described a lake, pine forests, and fruit orchards, as well as a burial site on a hill, where a statue and a picture of a deceased princess in a gilt frame, was encased in wood and covered with cloth. She also described a burial cellar.

> There were sarcophagi with mummies of the Royal Family. My father opened one up to show me. There was an old lady, very elaborately dressed. I remember it well.

Hymie, my mother's brother, and six years her senior, told his children that the estate – which was in an area called Byutichik – was owned by a Polish Count, Pau Pippin.

Despite the discrepancy of the identity of the owner, both siblings recounted a life of abundance and joy, living in the grounds of the estate, and fishing on the lake.

The estate had associated tracts of land which were leased out to local farmers, and in addition to looking after the grounds, her father (and his father before him) leased a piece of land and farmed on it. The excess produce was sold at the weekly market in a small nearby town – Malat – and in time, he saved enough money and was able to buy a piece of land in that town, for the family.

The estate owner also gifted the family a piece of the forest, and allowed my grandfather to cut down the trees, in order to build a house for himself. According to my mother, her father did not want a wooden house, so was given special permission to sell the trees and use the proceeds to build a brick house instead. My mother described with much delight the fact that he had built a double-storey house with no building knowledge, so that the walls upstairs had no weight-bearing walls for support beneath them and were consequently buckled. But it was nonetheless an impressive home, comprising three upstairs apartments as well as a restaurant and bakery downstairs, run by her mother.

That home is still standing in Malat today. It has a name plaque that was recently installed by the Department of Cultural Heritage in Lithuania. It reads, in Yiddish and Lithuanian: 'Isaac Charif's House'.

While they were still living on the estate (in Byutichik), their family home was in an area contested by three warring countries – Lithuania, Poland and Russia. The borders kept changing, armies came and went, and the local Jews often bore the brunt of the ruling army's brutality. The Lithuanians were particularly aggressive, justifying their cruelty with the stated belief that the Jews were communists who had helped sell out the country to the Russians.

There were stories my mother told of soldiers who would ransack their home, taking whatever they wanted. She recounted how some of these men, at one such occurrence, stole her mother's cutlery and candlesticks – pondering the worth of the good silver versus the old cutlery where age had exposed the base metal. It amused her to no end that eventually they had chosen to take the worn-out old cutlery believing, wrongly, that the base metal was gold.

More than once, my grandfather was taken away by Polish or Lithuanian soldiers. Once, when his horse and cart came back without him, the family thought he had been killed. Eventually they found that he had escaped into the surrounding woods and gone into hiding at the home of his sister-in-law.

On another occasion Polish 'partisans' arrived at their home and tormented him. They threw a hand grenade over his head, stole food (wrapping it in pages torn from his religious books, to insult him further) and left.

Believing they would return for him later, he once again hid in the forest for a few days, eventually making his way to Malat to a friend, who was a doctor there. The upper storey of the doctor's house was occupied by the General commanding the Polish forces in the town, and my grandfather must have had some standing within the community, because when he was introduced to the General and told him of his ordeal, the General gave him a letter forbidding any Polish soldier from harassing him and his family, and arranged an escort to take him home.

Soon after, they moved from the estate in Byutichik to the house he had built for his family in Malat.

***

My grandfather was instrumental in the lives of his children. He was the one who engaged a tutor for them to catch up their schooling after they had been ill, or after they had moved from Russian to Hebrew schools. He was the one who travelled by horse and cart to take them to, and fetch them from, school in a nearby town. He was the one who made all the practical decisions and doled out the punishment when they disobeyed. But he was not despotic – he generally consulted and negotiated with my mother on matters that were important to her.

My mother's recollections of her father were etched with a mix of reverence and love. She spoke of him as *'Daddy,'* addressing his memory in an endearing, informal and child-like way. She painted a picture of her father as a progressive man possessed of exceptional vision for the time in which they lived.

One of my mother's favourite stories about her father, was how she came home one Friday night – Shabbat had already commenced – and she unthinkingly lit a candle (which is strictly forbidden on the Sabbath) to go up the stairs. Maria – their long-term, non-Jewish maid – saw it and shouted at her, telling her that her bad behaviour would be reported to her father. My grandparents were religious and observed all the strict rules of Judaism, so she knew she was in trouble.

The next morning, she waited for him to punish her. She spent the next two days waiting for him to confront her – walking on eggshells all weekend – but he remained silent. Finally, before she left to go back to school, she took her father aside and confessed.

'I know', he said. 'Maria told me'. When she asked why he had omitted to punish her he smiled and said: 'You suffered all weekend anticipating the punishment, correct? That was your punishment. By saying nothing I punished you far more severely than if I had raised it'.

My mother never forgot this exchange, and talked of it whenever she was trying to explain her father's style of parenting, which, despite his traditional and prescriptive lifestyle, was imbued with a modern flexibility; a kind and thoughtful understanding of his daughter's needs – granting her equal rights to her brothers, and facilitating her aspirations, promoting her talents and encouraging her to go to university at a time when daughters generally did not even go to high-school.

He was – without doubt – the formative person in her life.

My grandmother, Rachel, (after whom I am named) played a different parenting role in my mother's life. By all accounts, they had a warm, traditional, mother-daughter relationship, typical of that era.

My mother described an incident to illustrate this. She arrived home from university sporting a sleek, short, modern hairdo, having cut off her striking long plaits in a fit of pique when they wouldn't fit under the hat she was planning to wear to a ball. Expecting her mother to be delighted with her new appearance, she was instead confronted by tears, her mother mourning for her 'beautiful child' who had – with a haircut – become an adult.

From my grandmother, my mother learned 'womanly skills' – her abundant culinary expertise, her love of cooking and baking, her success as a *Balabusta* (Yiddish homemaker), her accomplishment as a mother. These were characteristics she readily and frequently attributed to her adored mother's influence, for the rest of her life.

***

On a quiet weekend in June 1941, my grandfather was visiting his two daughters, in Kovno – the capital of

Lithuania. At that time, my mother was married and had a child, and lived with her family in Kovno. Her sister, Gita, lived and worked in Kovno, as well. My grandfather had come alone – my grandmother had remained at home in Malat, unable to leave the restaurant. On that Sunday, Lithuania was invaded by Germany.

> You can imagine – we were sitting peacefully on a Sunday, a sunny Sunday morning in June. Because Russia and Germany have got a non-aggression pact, and Lithuania is ruled by Russia, we think we are quite safe. But then, we see at about 12 o'clock in the morning, German planes attacking Kovno (that was the capital of Lithuania), bombs were all the time just booming – that is all that we heard. And from that very minute, we could already not get out into the street because we were straight away arrested, or taken away to be shot.
>
> Now I want to stress, when the first attack took place, it was not by the Germans – it was by the Lithuanians themselves, because they were – they had it against the Jews. They thought that the Jews are communists and the Jews sold Lithuania to Russia, to the communists, and now, this was their revenge. When the Germans came, everything was ready for the Germans. As soon as they came onto the skies – the German aeroplanes – the Lithuanians started to kill the Jews in the streets. Kill and torture and pour petrol onto them, and force water from a hose down their throats – whatever they could

do. Ten thousand Jews were killed by the Lithuanians – with the German's help. And now, with hindsight, we know that the Germans had already a fifth column in Lithuania, and as soon as they attacked Lithuania, the Lithuanians themselves, did what they did.

My mother, her husband (Mokka), child (Michael) and mother-in-law, as well as my mother's sister, Gita, and their father – immediately went into hiding in a cellar on the outskirts of Kovno, at the home of a relative. They remained there, huddled together and in shock, for a few days.

After the initial carnage perpetrated by the Lithuanians in those first few days settled down, the surviving Jews were forced out of hiding, rounded up and confined to the Ghetto.

Gita worked as a book-keeper in a factory in Kovno at the time. In order to help her avoid going into the Ghetto, her non-Jewish work colleagues secured coveted seats for her and my grandfather to travel back to Malat by bus. Despite my mother's pleas for her to stay with them in Kovno, Gita wanted to go home to be with her parents.

My grandparents and their two younger children were later murdered by the Nazis – on a single day, the entire Jewish population of Malat was rounded up and shot, their bodies dumped into a mass grave dug into what used to be the children's football field.

Many years later, a letter (translated from Yiddish and transcribed below) serendipitously came into my mother's hands, chillingly describing the fate of the Jews of Malat – including my grandparents.

> *Dear Moshe, Beni, Bella and children. Remain all well and we shall pray for you in Heaven. Pay the one who will forward to you this note. We are fasting two days and we shall soon be going to the slaughter. The Memorial Day of our death will be 29th August, you should observe it. Your father is not at home – he is probably not alive anymore. He was taken away with all the men of the town. All the women and children are locked up in the synagogues. We are kept here while our communal grave is being dug. The children and we all are suffering very much until our death.*

It was written in Yiddish by a woman who lived in Malat, to her brother, and then thrown out of the synagogue window. The letter was picked up by a Lithuanian woman who had known them, and she kept the letter, unsure of what to do with it, but was somehow aware of its significance. Twenty years later, a group of Holocaust survivors came back to visit Malat and the Lithuanian woman gave one of them the letter she had secreted for all those years.

The letter was sent to the writer's brother, who had migrated to South Africa before the war. He in turn gave it to my mother – at the time she was the Chairlady of the *Malater Society* (an organisation established for survivors from Malat). She had it translated, and sent the original to Yad Vashem, the Holocaust Museum in Israel.

CHAPTER 2.
MOKKA

(LITHUANIA, PRE-1945)

Lea and Mokka, Kovno, 1937

I am six years old, riffling through my mother's easily-unlocked dressing table drawer. I come across a photo of my much-younger mother enfolded in the arms of a handsome man. He is NOT my father.

They are both smiling, and the chemistry between them is palpable, even to my inexperienced eyes. I am stunned and affronted. Forgetting that I am trespassing in her drawer, I haul the photo off to accuse my mother.

'Who is this?' I demand.

Lea and Mokka (Moses) Klompus were married in Kovno, Lithuania, on 22 May 1937.

By all accounts, he was the love of her life.

She was almost 23 years old, and had met him the year before when he agreed to teach her the skills that she needed to take a potential secretarial job at a film company, that never eventuated. A week after meeting her, he told her he had fallen in love with her and wanted to marry her.

He was a tall, good looking, educated man, who had studied and taught at Konigsberg University in Germany. In 1933 he had left Konigsberg and moved to Kovno. He'd had a problem with his vocal cords, and had given up teaching – becoming instead a 'Correspondent' at the Commerce Bank in Kovno, where his fluency in many languages enabled him to communicate with banks in various countries.

A year after they got married, their son Michael was born. At some point, Mokka's mother came to live with them in their apartment in Kovno. My mother never spoke ill of her mother-in-law, but I got the distinct impression there was no love lost between them from the occasional disdainful comments she made in passing.

She fried Mokka pork schnitzel in butter! *(Presumably, this was before they married, and not in my mother's kosher home, where both pork, and meat and dairy served together, were always strictly forbidden).*

> When I was in labour and walking to the hospital to give birth, she walked behind me along the street, as if she did not know me!

After Lithuania was occupied by Germany, the family moved into the Kovno Ghetto, where even though life was very hard, they managed to remain together.

A feature of life in the Ghetto was an intermittent *selektion*, when everyone was forced to line up on the *appelplatz* (assembly area), and they were 'randomly' allocated to one or other side. Those on one side were allowed to return to 'normal' life, and the others were removed – sometimes sent away to a death camp, sometimes marched to a nearby forest and shot, sometimes taken to the Ninth Fort (a fort in northern Kovno originally used as a prison, but after German occupation, used as a place of execution for Jews).

During one infamous *selektion* in the Kovno Ghetto, 10,000 people were sent away, and later murdered on a single day. At that *selektion*, not knowing what fate held in store, or why they were being forced to line up on the *appelplatz*, Mokka, Lea, Mokka's mother and Michael, stood together as a family. At that stage they didn't yet know that people who were younger or appeared strong and healthy, were less likely to be selected to be sent away. But intuitively my mother tried to make her mother-in-law look younger.

> I was busy putting a colourful scarf over her head to hide her grey hair, and rubbing some red paper over

her cheeks that she shouldn't look so pale and old, but she was just busy scratching bits of stuck cement off Mokka's coat.

The camp leader was standing in front, with a little stick, and pointing. He was standing in front and as we were coming – the family – he was pointing, dividing families – half here, half there, half here, half there – pointing with his little stick where to go. We didn't know what was the left side and what was the right side, whether this is good or that is good, we didn't know what it meant. At that stage we didn't know what is going on. Police were standing on both sides – these were the Jewish police, the Ghetto police. They took away a whole family with three small children standing in front of me, to the left. And as I came towards him – I was there holding my child, there was my husband and my mother-in-law – I don't even remember that I saw him, and I just pulled to the right side and went to that side. I don't know how this happened, or even what happened, but we all four went through. And that's how they were sorting out and sorting out and sorting out until the afternoon. And in the afternoon, apparently they got tired, and they just surrounded the balance, the young and the old and all of them, and took them all away. Took them all away. But we remained together in the Ghetto.

Against all odds, they continued to live together in the Ghetto for fifteen months. They survived *selektions*, hunger and brutality – my mother and Mokka working, and her mother-in-law looking after the infant Michael, until October 1942 when the Nazi authorities issued a demand for 2,000 able-bodied men from the Ghetto to be sent to Estonia. The *Judenraht* (Jewish Council) provided a list and Mokka's name was on it. There was an offer for the men's families to go with them – if they agreed, they were promised that they could continue to live together. Mokka had no option – he had been selected and had to leave – but Lea and her mother-in-law had a choice to make. It was a difficult decision – by then the Jews of Kovno's Ghetto already knew that they couldn't trust what they were being told. Still, after much agonising, they decided to go to Estonia together with Mokka.

> Were they really transporting us to a new camp, or are they sending us for extermination? We were deliberating and deliberating and eventually we decided we are all four going together. If they are killing us, they kill all four of us and be done with it. If they leave us alone, to live and continue, so we continue and struggle through, waiting for the war to be finished.

On 26 October 1942, they turned up for transportation to Estonia, as a family. But as soon as they reached the meeting point, by the railway, they were separated. My mother was sent to be 'processed' before being sent to

MOKKA

Vaivara concentration camp, in Estonia. Mokka was sent to a camp in an unknown location, and Lea's mother-in-law and son Michael, aged four at the time, were sent together to Auschwitz, in Poland.

She never saw her child again.

In most of her interviews, my mother ends at this point, saying 'This was the last time I saw my loved ones alive.' But in one interview, she details how she and Mokka did, in fact, meet again.

***

In the Vaivara concentration camp, my mother had managed to impress the camp leader – the Lager Fuhrer – with her abilities, and he had placed her in charge of running the barracks. When she subsequently became ill with typhus, he personally arranged for her to attend the local medical facility, insisting she be given the chance to get better, rather than be sent to Auschwitz. But then, while she was in the medical facility, Vaivara was closed. All the inmates – except for those in the medical facility, who were simply left to die – and all the staff (including the *Lager Fuhrer*) were transferred to another concentration camp, Erida.

My mother was miraculously rescued from the medical facility with the help of some friends, and was transferred from Vaivara to Erida, only to find herself once again in the 'sick camp' – a place where ill people from all the camps in Estonia were gathered together before being transferred to Auschwitz. Having quickly established that this place was simply a waiting room for transportation to certain death, my mother was determined to get out.

> I was already better and I was going out, out of the barrack, and rubbing myself with snow all the time and walking around a bit and going to see what was happening all around and about. Two weeks later the camp is getting fuller and fuller so I got to talk to the *Sanitater*. The *Sanitater* was a Croatian in the SS guards, and he was going around in all the camps, in all the men's and women's camps wherever they were, and bringing the sick people to that camp. He told me that when there were over a thousand, they were sent away. And I see that the camp is filling up and filling up and filling up. So I decided I am not going away with them to Auschwitz. I have to get out of here.

Erida comprised two distinct camps – a 'sick camp' and a 'working camp'. The two camps were located on two small hills, separated by a gully. There was a bridge crossing the gully, with guards posted at the entrance to the bridge. Anyone entering or leaving the sick camp had to have an entry permit, which they presented to the guards. For many days, my mother watched the comings and goings, trying to work out how to get a permit to cross the bridge to the other camp where, as long as she could work, she had a chance to survive. Eventually she devised a plan.

There was a doctor in the healthy camp – he was coming with a nurse every morning to the sick camp. He didn't have medicine to give us, but he was coming to ask how you are, or to tell something. He was a friend of mine, because when I studied in Kovno, he was studying medicine and I was studying science, and the first two years we were doing chemistry together at the chemistry department there, and we became good friends.

So I said to him, ' Listen, I have to get out from here and you are the one that can help me'. I said – 'I've been watching you. When you are going through that little gate between this camp and that camp, there is a guard. The guard sees that you are in a white overall, and the nurse with you is in a white overall with a syringe, he doesn't even ask for your permit. So, come one day with your nurse, and let her give me her overall with her syringe, and I'll go back with you, and she can go back with her permit card'. And he agreed to help me – despite the risk. And the plan worked.

As I walked over the bridge, and as I came into the camp, I saw the three men in charge of the camp – the *Lager Fuhrer*, the *Yiddish Lager Fuhrer* and the *Arbeit's Inspektor* (the works inspector). Protocol was that one should only approach the *Arbeit's Inspektor*, but I went directly to the *Lager Fuhrer*. He was a terrible man – I saw him give a man a glass of 'Lysol' to drink once, and I saw him smile as that man suffered and died in agony – but to me he was very good. I said, '*Herr Lager Fuhrer*, you promised me work when I was well, and I am well'. He kept his word, and organised for me to go and work in the kitchen.

In time, on the orders of the *Lager Fuhrer*, my mother took over the running of the kitchen. In this capacity, she maintained contact with the *Sanitater* (who had provided her the information about her fate, had she remained in the 'sick camp'), offering him tea and food whenever he arrived, frozen, in her kitchen. Eventually, she took a chance, and asked him to look for her husband, whom she believed was in one of the men's camps. When he found Mokka, my mother convinced the *Sanitater* – even though he was an SS guard – to deliver a note to her husband, and then to bring him to Erida.

He brought him. When I saw him, he was black as coal, the face – black as coal, I am telling you. I used to warm water in the night, when the kitchen was already closed, and everybody was already gone home, and the camp guards were not there. There was a small little room at the side I used. I used to take him in there and wash him and scrub him and scrub him, until I scrubbed him to his skin. Until he became more normal. And I gave him food, you know – he was already looking more human.

Then I spoke to the *Lager Fuhrer*. I said to him, my husband is here. My husband speaks German, he was educated at the Konigsberg University, and all that, can't you give him some work in the office? One day, the *Lager Fuhrer* came around and I called my husband in and they spoke. The *Lager Fuhrer* told him that he should sweep there around the blocks, do something outside and if he will need him in the office for interpreting something, he will call him. So, my husband was there, he had recovered – he was alright – and then he got sick with typhus. We were not allowed to go and visit them – but I would steal in after work, to go and see him in the sick room. He didn't recognize me or anything, but later, he got better.

He was in the men's camp at Erida and I in the women's. I saw to it that he has got shoes. I got for him a jacket there, some decent clothes. And then, Erida had to be closed and we had to move again. They moved us to an empty field, called Lagedy where they made a temporary camp. The women were separate, and the men were in another place but close by. We were not long there, about a month, and from there they put us on a boat, and we came to Stutthof. So I was with my husband on that boat, until we came to Stutthof.

By the time I got to the camp in Stutthof, my husband was already in a men's camp again, barefoot again. In Erida I could look after him, but in Stutthof, he's already barefoot again. He used to come to the wire, through the wire we could talk. What happened to your shoes? He said 'Well, they've stolen them'.

There, in Stutthof, there some Polish men had a workshop for shoes. I gave them some of the bread – there we used to get bread – so I gave them some bread, and they gave me a pair of nice leather shoes. I gave it to him. I threw it over, the shoes, and I used to throw him over some of my bread that I used to get.

From Stutthof, they used to send away groups for work in places where work is needed. I didn't want to stay in Stutthof, and I had registered to go and work. I had told my husband also to register, for work somewhere. We arranged that if we both survived, we should try to meet in Konigsberg, because in Konigsberg he had friends from before the war. And that was left like that and I went away to work.

I was sent away to Ochsenzoll – to the ammunitions factory. On the way we were travelling in an open carriage and I saw my husband in a potato field. He was there with some people working, and I saw him. I saw him straight away and he was looking – it was quite far – he was looking, looking where I was and when I came past, he just made a farewell gesture.

That's the last that I remember of him.

CHAPTER 3.
MICHAEL

(LITHUANIA, 1938–1943)

Lea, Michael and Mokka, Kovno, 1939

It is 4 a.m. on the morning of their arrival into Bergen-Belsen. Everyone in the train carriage believes they are going to die. Quietly the women begin to disclose intimacies – akin to confessions at the last rites. One talks of her inadequacies as a wife, another of her failure to give charity. A third tells of her meanness.

My mother, however, has no regrets. She says she

bought her child the most expensive Czech leather shoes available.

He was four years old when the Nazis separated him from his parents and sent him to Auschwitz.

MICHAEL

Michael was born on the 7th June 1938, to Lea and Mokka, one year after they were married. A framed photograph of him – a chubby nude baby of about five months old, lying on his tummy on a blanket – graced the mantelpiece of my childhood home.

This was the only image I had of my mother's baby who was killed during the Holocaust. I didn't ever think of him as anything else – he was simply a named baby who was lost among so many other relatives who were lost during that time.

And then, about two years ago, I received an e-mail from a stranger – she said she was a distant cousin. She asked for information about 'Your mother's little boy who perished. In Kovno Ghetto we played together. I do not remember his name.'

Instantly, that two-dimensional photograph of a baby was transformed into a real little boy – a child who played. A toddler who learned to crawl and walk and talk and express his thoughts and feelings and fears. A little boy who probably experienced hunger and anguish. Who wore the most expensive Czech leather shoes his mother could buy.

A fully aware four-year-old who was separated forcibly from his mother and father and sent, with his paternal grandmother, on separate transportation to Auschwitz, where he was murdered.

I do not allow my mind to correlate this child with other precious children in my life. The thought is too painful and too traumatic to even contemplate.

I don't know how my mother bore this, her greatest loss. I don't know how she held future children and grandchildren in her arms without disintegrating – but she did. She held us and loved us and cherished us.

And she very, very seldom spoke of Michael, other than in the abstract terms of a 'baby lost'.

My mother's oldest grandson bears his name, as does her youngest great-grandchild. Children in two generations have been named for his memory, so that all his potential as a real human being, a little boy who played, can be perpetuated.

CHAPTER 4.
HYMIE

(LITHUANIA AND SOUTH AFRICA, 1908–1996)

Hymie

We are both at Cheder in Malat. Our parents are still in Byutishik, but Lea and I are living in the partly completed house that our father is building in Malat. During the term, we attend school there and share the upstairs with the many rats resident there. I am dead-scared of them and often creep into Lea's bed at night to avoid them. Lea is not afraid of anything *or anybody. One night, a rat gets entangled in her hair and she just gets the rat loose, throws it down into the street and returns to bed and settles down for the night. I light a candle, and remain awake all night, vigilant for further rat intruders. She sleeps unperturbed.*

(From a letter written by Hymie for his children)

From my earliest memory, there was nobody on earth who my mother loved more than her older brother, Hymie. Perhaps it was because he was the only sibling who escaped the Holocaust; perhaps it was because he was the only surviving member of her nuclear family that remained; perhaps it was because of the early closeness of their relationship before the war. But there was no question that on the list of people that my mother loved, he came first.

They grew up very close to each other. Even though there were six years between them, they formed one unit. They were schooled together, first at home, and later in Malat. Initially Hymie was a few years ahead of her, but she soon caught up and joined him. When he first went to Hebrew school in Malat, he boarded with friends, but once she joined him, they lived together in the house their father was building. Every Friday they used to walk home together to their parents in Byutichik – a distance of 14 miles – and then back on a Sunday evening. They socialised together, and shared friends. Eventually Hymie went to a Yeshiva in Wilkomir for two years, and then went to a private college there that Lea also attended.

In 1926, Hymie decided to leave school. He explained to me that his decision was based on a traumatic event where his father, coming to pay the tuition fees in a heavy snowstorm, had an accident where the horse cart broke. He struggled through the snow, manually dragging the cart, arriving with badly swollen and bleeding hands. This was too much for the sensitive Hymie.

He said: 'I cried like a baby after my father left, and decided I would never allow my father to repeat this ordeal on my behalf. I would never again allow my dad to go through such a heart-breaking and bloody task'.

At that time, many Jews from Lithuania had migrated to South Africa, drawn by the economic prosperity afforded by the Gold Rush, and by the relative freedom from religious persecution that life in South Africa offered. Family members of both my grandmother, Rachel and my grandfather, Isaac, had migrated to South Africa before the war, and there were many aunts, uncles and cousins living in various South African cities.

My mother's maternal grandparents, Joseph and Nachama Isaacson, had immigrated to South Africa, to a small town, Dordrecht, in the Cape Province, some years before.

Hymie applied to go and live with his grandparents, and received immigration papers in August 1926. He left for South Africa almost immediately. It was a very traumatic and emotional parting from his family, and especially, as he described it, 'from my beloved Lea'. He didn't know it at the time, but he would never see his parents and two youngest siblings again.

But in the middle of 1946, against all odds, he was reunited with my mother.

***

My mother was liberated on 15 April 1945 from Bergen-Belsen, after five weeks in that death camp, and almost three years in various other concentration camps. She credited her survival in Bergen-Belsen to her time in the preceding concentration camp, Ochsenzoll, where she was part of an involuntary labour force for an ammunition factory. There, she said, the inmates had been fed a little better, and slept a little better, which enabled them to build some reserves to withstand the horrific conditions they encountered in Bergen-Belsen.

> No work, no food, no place to move – mountains of dead bodies who were thrown out of the windows of the barracks every day, piled into hills outside, covered in snow. And typhus infestation that was uncontrollable.

My mother was fluent in many languages – Lithuanian, Russian, Polish, Estonian, Hebrew, German and Yiddish, (in later years she added French and Afrikaans) and she was fairly fluent in English. Her language skills helped her throughout her time in the concentration camps – being able to address the *Lager Fuhrer* or other Nazi authorities in German, almost certainly gave her a subliminal advantage in all her dealings with them.

Similarly, her ability to speak English enabled her to negotiate with officials in the British Army a day after liberation, to move the relatively well women who had come from Ochsenzoll, into the newly-vacated barracks where the German *Blitzwomen* (SS guards who had controlled the concentration camps) had been living, so as to avoid the typhus that was ravaging everyone else in the camp.

As soon as the women were transferred, and she knew they were all safe, she allowed herself the 'luxury' of succumbing to illness, and remained unconscious in a sick bay for three weeks.

When she recovered, she began to work as a private secretary to the Commanding Officer of Bergen-Belsen – that by then had become a displaced person's camp. In that capacity, she made friends with a Jewish sergeant who was working in the office. He travelled to London every month to report to the government in Britain. My mother remembered Hymie's address in South Africa, and on his visits to London, the sergeant set about contacting him on her behalf.

Hymie, at the same time, was desperately looking for her (and the rest of the family), hoping against hope that they had survived. Somehow the connection was made, and one year and three months after liberation, my mother emigrated to South Africa.

She had, in fact, been offered passage to Israel. At that time, a Jewish Brigade was formed to assist with the illegal immigration of Jews to what would become Israel. People from that Brigade came to Bergen-Belsen, offering to assist survivors with planning for their future, and especially with facilitating migration to Israel.

Although my mother had always dreamed of going to Israel, and most of the surviving women she had befriended in the camps went there, in the end, her bond to her brother outweighed her Zionist desire.

```
Memorandum

From:- B.R.C. Office,              To:- Miss Livingstone,
       Att. Search Bureau,              B.R.C. & O. St. John,
       C.C.G.(B.E.),                    c/o H.Q. Mil. Gov.,
       21 Funde, B.A.O.R.               BELSEN, Concentration Camp.

W/HIS                                   21st December, 1945.

          Lea KLOMPUS, Kuche 3, Belsen Camp.

       We are informed by our London Headquarters that they
forwarded a liberation form to Belsen on 1st September, 1945,
with the information that Hymie Cherif was trying to arrange
for her entry into South Africa. They have now received a
cable from the South African Red Cross, Johannesburg which
reads as follows:-
       "OCWR 1109 Please advise Lea Klompus entry permit granted
        this country. Contact British Authorities."

       We should be most grateful if you could contact this
person, and give her this information.
                                    for Evelyn Bark.
```

Letter advising my mother that her entry permit to South Africa was granted.

***

One of my mother's first cousins in South Africa, (her father's brother's son) was David Burgin, an influential lawyer with connections to the South African government. Despite South Africa not allowing Holocaust survivors to migrate there, strings were pulled to grant her a tourist visa to South Africa from Lourenco Marques, a Portuguese colony, (now Mozambique), adjacent to South Africa. She thus went first to Portugal, from where she travelled by boat to Lourenco Marques.

David and his brother Ivan were waiting in Lourenco Marques to carry her off the boat – a reunion that none of them ever forgot. Soon after that, she arrived in South Africa, where she was reunited with Hymie. David, meanwhile, set about the task of obtaining a permanent residence permit for her – which was granted in July 1947.

For the rest of her life in South Africa, Hymie was an integral part. There was a bond and a closeness between them that exceeded words or deeds. She consulted with him on most matters – allowing him to have an opinion, and giving him the courtesy of her decisions before she enacted them – which was considerably more leeway than she generally gave others. He mattered more than anyone else.

When we were growing up, our family and Hymie's lived in adjacent small towns on the East Rand. They visited most Sundays. We spent most Jewish holidays together – my mother cooking up a storm and transporting it all to their home, where Hymie delighted in complimenting her profusely on her culinary skills, reminiscent of their mother's.

Hymie's children were as important to her as her own. The last document she signed – two months before she died – facilitated his daughter's migration to Australia.

My mother truly adored her brother, and absorbed him and his children into the tight circle of her nearest and dearest, until the day she died.

CHAPTER 5.
SAMUEL

(LITHUANIA AND SOUTH AFRICA, 1910–1976)

Lea and Samuel on their Wedding Day, 1948

Sixty-six-year-old Samuel – my father – is lying on his deathbed in ICU in the Johannesburg General Hospital. My mother sits at the foot of the bed, trying unsuccessfully to warm his icy feet. She looks up at me mournfully.

'I am losing my best friend', she says. Her choice of words speaks volumes. Not her love, not her soulmate, not her husband of 28 years, but her best friend.

Their relationship has always been complicated.

SAMUEL

In April 1948 – less than two years after arriving in South Africa – my mother married Samuel Leibowitz, my father.

They were introduced by a mutual acquaintance, at a Yiddish writers meeting, in Johannesburg. She had been invited to be the guest speaker, talking about her Holocaust experiences. My father was an aspiring writer – a sensitive and romantic soul – and it didn't take much for him to be smitten by my mother, as captivated by her beauty as he was by the tragedy that enveloped her. For the rest of his life, he sought to put her on a pedestal – casting her in his mind as a fragile refugee that needed protecting from the horrors of the past.

'Don't upset Mummy', he would whisper to us. 'Don't make her sad. She has had so much heartache already'.

But he was ill-equipped to deal with her, mostly because his image of her couldn't be further from the truth. She was a strong, exceptionally intelligent and self-sufficient woman who had survived the Holocaust in large part because of her steely determination and pragmatism. These were the enduring qualities she brought to the table – to her marriage, her family, her community, her life, but which had no connection to his idealized image of her as a needy waif.

My father was also from Lithuania. He was born in a small town, Ponevez, in 1910, the youngest of five siblings. His father, a pharmacist, owned his own pharmacy. At the outbreak of the first world war, the family had fled to Russia, where they were refugees in Vitebst. There, the older brothers and sisters attended school, and when they returned to Ponevez, they continued in secular schools and the two older brothers were eventually sent to University – one to Berne, in Switzerland, and the other, to Brunn, in Belgium.

My father, however, was sent to *Yeshiva*, (Jewish religious seminary) to fulfill his own father's thwarted dream of becoming a Rabbi. But as a teenager, he began secretly to read 'enlightened' books which were forbidden in the *Yeshiva*. Thus began his life-long conflict with religion, and also, his life-long love of literature.

In 1929, at the age of 19, Samuel's father sent him to live with his paternal uncle Uriah and his wife Dinah, in South Africa. Whether this was an economic decision – to earn and send money home – or a measure intent on protecting him from the increasing anti-Jewish sentiment in Lithuania at the time, he never knew. But his parents' decision caused a bitter conflict inside of him that he carried with him for the rest of his life – anger that he had been sent away, and guilt that it had saved his life (both his parents were later killed in the Holocaust).

On arrival in South Africa, he spent three months in East London, a coastal town in the Eastern Cape Province, with his uncle and aunt, during which time he learnt basic English. Soon after, he was sent away to work as a server in an eating house, in a remote corner of the Transkei, in a village known as Tsolo. Almost the entire population of Tsolo was dark-skinned, native people, with whom he had no commonality, and no shared language. There was no like-minded person with whom to share his feelings. He was isolated, lonely and afraid.

It was a traumatic time for Samuel.

He was angry with his father for having sent him to South Africa, and at the same time, he was bitterly homesick. It was impossible for him to practise the religion he had spent his entire life studying, and he was terrified of the consequences of not doing so. Aside from his mother and sisters, he had never been exposed to women, and he had lived until that time in an almost exclusively Jewish setting. Now, he found himself transplanted into a new world that was completely alien – composed almost entirely of black African non-Jewish men and women – a world he never knew existed, and that he had never been prepared for.

Samuel had no secular knowledge on which to draw, and no tools to help him deal with the foreign environment in which he found himself. He lacked innate adaptability, and the emotional scars from this period endured for the rest of his life, almost certainly presenting in later years as depression.

Eventually, things improved.

Like my mother, my father had a natural talent for languages, and quickly learned to speak Afrikaans as well as several of the indigenous languages of South Africa. Because this was unusual – a European Jew speaking Afrikaans and black languages – it gave him confidence, and enhanced his ability to interact with a variety of people. He began writing prolifically, documenting his thoughts and feelings, and astutely describing the people and events he witnessed daily.

He never wrote in English, which he described as a cold and soulless language, preferring Yiddish and Afrikaans, with their warm, descriptive nuances. Some of his stories found their way into Afrikaans newspapers, including *'Die Vaderland'* – a mainstream nationalistic and anti-Semitic newspaper at the time.

The editor had read one of his stories and offered to publish a series under a pseudonym, finding his typically Jewish surname too 'offensive'. My father stood his ground, insisting that if his 'Jew-created' stories were good enough, so too was his name. The series was eventually published, weekly, under the identifiably Jewish by-line of 'Samuel Leibowitz'.

His circle of friends grew, and by 1934 he had moved from the remote Transkei to the more central, bustling Transvaal, living and working in various 'concession stores' in small mining towns close to Johannesburg.

This, then, was the young man that my mother met. He didn't quite fit her previous criteria – she preferred tall men – he was 5'4; she revered education – he had no secular schooling; she was sophisticated – and he was in no way worldly. But he was sensitive, funny, intelligent, caring and kind. They had both lost their parents and extended family in the Holocaust, and they had both been transported from 'home' in Lithuania, and cast into a new, foreign life in South Africa.

Samuel also had one more draw card – my mother knew both his brothers. They had been her teachers at high school in Wilkomir; the older of his brothers had, in fact been her principal. Knowing his siblings gave her a solid connection to his background. It gave her the added security she sought.

By the time my mother met him, my father was already quite accomplished as a Yiddish writer, with a number of published stories. But writing stories did not pay the rent, so he continued to work as a salesman in various retail businesses – a petrol station, a bicycle shop, and various concession stores.

After some time, he had saved up enough money to open up his own shop – the Grootvlei Filling Station and Cycle Store – in a small town about 50 miles from Johannesburg. But my father was not a natural businessman – his true love was writing – and he had no real interest in, or flair for commerce. The venture – and one that came after it – failed.

Still, he persevered, remaining a 'shop-keeper' for the rest of his life, and eventually his business succeeded despite him – in no small measure because my mother was there to rescue it.

By the time I was born in 1954, my parents were living in Benoni, a small town on the East Rand, 30 miles from Johannesburg, and my father had a shop in Elandsfontein, another small town close by. It started off as a bicycle shop – the Springbok Cycle Agency – although it eventually transformed into a general goods store, selling everything from bicycle parts to clothing, to music, to batteries, to shoemakers' leather, to crockery and air rifles – more or less anything and everything, that was non-perishable. It was forever known to us simply as 'The Shop'.

The Shop was located across the road from the Elandsfontein rail station, in an industrial area, and catered almost exclusively to the black workers who travelled through the station to and from the nearby factories and goldmines. The workers were paid weekly on a Friday, and so on Friday afternoon and Saturday morning, The Shop became a sea of mainly black men buying clothing and other commodities to take home to their families. I can remember as a child in primary school, walking to the station and catching two trains – on my own – to get to The Shop on a Friday afternoon, when my sister and I were expected to help.

When it was still just a bicycle shop, my mother asked the resident salesman/mechanic/security guard – Ben – to teach her to take apart and rebuild bicycles. She quickly learned to identify every single part, and became adept at fixing faulty brakes and gears and fitting tyres and wheels, in no time. These skills stayed with her forever. I remember walking into her apartment when she was an old lady, to find her exercise bike in pieces on a towel placed on the carpeted floor, while she oiled, greased and reconstructed it.

Although The Shop provided well for the family, my father felt enslaved to it. He turned up begrudgingly, five and a half days a week, sitting at the shop's makeshift kitchen, drinking tea and reading his newspaper. The radio permanently played the news and the Stock Exchange report, while he kept an occasional eye on the sales staff. The only shop-related thing he enjoyed was when the travelling salesmen paid their visit, and they could sit and have tea, or a 'schnapps' together, and tell jokes and stories.

***

My father was a wonderful storyteller. When we were young, we would go for neighbourhood walks, and he would tell us stories about the everyday things around us. He especially loved nature, constantly pointing out its wonder, beauty and quirks – stopping to pick flowers or track a butterfly.

I remember how an old garage door we regularly passed came to life as he described it as a young tree, then took us on a journey through its life cycle until it ended up as a manufactured and decaying old garage door hanging on a hinge, waiting to succumb to age and disuse.

He was also a natural comedian – he instinctively knew how to deliver a punchline, or physically contort his face or body to get a laugh. He had a keen eye, a quick wit, and a wicked sense of humour. So many of his 'verbal caricatures' (mostly in Yiddish) still resonate in my memory today. Though he played no instrument, he had a refined appreciation for music, and a good ear – inevitably pointing out a discordant note as he lay on the couch listening as my sister practised the piano.

Sunday morning, in our home, was generally a fun time. My mom would cook, and my dad would entertain. He would commonly haul out his tape recorder, and fool around translating a passage from the Hebrew bible before him into one African language and then another, to the amazement of our Zulu maid. Or he would tap out an entire melody with both hands on his perfect white teeth, or find some other way to amuse us.

Our parents did not go out much. Every now and then there would be an outing to Yiddish theatre, or a film, or the very occasional celebratory dinner at a kosher restaurant in Johannesburg (usually following my mother's graduation or some other achievement). On the odd occasion that they did go to the theatre, we would typically get a hilarious follow-up version the next morning, when my father would re-create for us the stories or music. I clearly remember one Sunday morning when my short and portly father came to breakfast sporting a tablecloth tied seductively across one shoulder, singing opera. They had been out the night before to see a visiting Israeli opera star, and this was his impromptu impersonation of her outfit and repertoire.

He may not have had a secular education, but it was my father who taught my sister and me to appreciate music, art and theatre.

As he got older, it became more and more obvious that my father was not happy. His aspirations as a writer never came to fruition and as time went by, he wrote less and less. There were few new stories after 1948, although after his death, my mother did publish some of his early work in an anthology of translated Yiddish stories written by various South African Yiddish writers. His hilarious antics got more and more infrequent, and he seemed ever more burdened by The Shop, and ever more vocal about the futility of his existence. He spent more time alone in his room reading the newspapers. It took more effort to cajole him to participate in family things – his mildly antisocial behaviour becoming increasingly accentuated with each passing year.

All the while, my mother continued doing whatever she did. She was independent, and she never let my father stop her from doing what she set out to do. If he would not accompany her to a meeting, she went alone. If there was a film she wanted to see, and he refused to go, she went with friends. If he stayed in his room most Sunday afternoons when her brother came to visit, she would only insist he put in a short appearance, forgiving his behaviour as 'tiredness from a hard week's work'. In many ways she simply ignored his protests, which only served to further facilitate his withdrawal.

In parallel, my mother took on more and more responsibility for The Shop. She did a book-keeping course to deal with the accounts. She drove to the wholesalers, in Johannesburg, to purchase stock. She learnt from friends who had successful businesses and expanded the range of goods for sale. She shared with these business friends joint co-operative purchasing, to keep costs down, and she made The Shop – almost single-handedly – succeed. As with everything else they shared, my mother's success left my father conflicted – grateful, but at the expense of his self-esteem.

My father was totally impractical. He couldn't change a light bulb, or connect a plug. He couldn't boil an egg, or make a sandwich. He never drove a car – walking or catching trains when my mother wasn't around to drive him.

In contrast, my mother could – and did – do everything. She could dismantle a broken mix-master, and it would work again. She used to maintain the primitive filter of our backyard swimming pool, ensuring it worked perfectly by measuring the water balance in the various sand layers, using a shoelace! She ran the household, doing all the accounts and the banking. She kept the garden, pruning the fruit trees and the roses. The car – and car maintenance – was her responsibility too.

In parenting, as with most other areas in their life, my parents were never a team. They approached the task of raising children with two opposing philosophies. My mother's premise was – 'I didn't have something, so I'll make sure my children do'. My father's premise was – 'I didn't have it, so neither will my children'. If we wanted something, we asked my mother. If we asked my father and he said no, we asked her anyway. And as with most other elements in her life, her decisions simply overrode his. My mother always won.

When I was eleven, my mother decided to attend a Holocaust seminar in Israel. She planned to be away for eight weeks. My father tried everything to stop her going, but every obstacle he put in her way, she overcame. She organised extra staff for The Shop. She planned meals with our resident nanny, who in any event cooked and managed the house. She organised school lifts for us, created chemist and butcher accounts to which we had access, and did everything possible to ensure her absence would not impact on our lives. In any case, we were independent children – in her day to day life my mother was seldom home, working or studying most days, so we were used to being on our own, getting around by bicycle and catching trains to work in The Shop on a Friday afternoon.

The last desperate hurdle my father threw up to try and scuttle my mother's planned trip to Israel was that he couldn't (or wouldn't) do the books for The Shop, and eight weeks was too long to leave the accounts unpaid. Undeterred, she came up with a unique solution: she taught me to manage the accounts. Thus, as a primary school child, for two months, I kept the books for The Shop. I checked the invoices, calculated and subtracted the discounts, wrote the checks, (which my father duly signed), added handwritten explanatory notes to accompany the payments and addressed and posted them to each of the wholesalers with whom she dealt. In retrospect, I wonder what their accounts department thought, when they saw the childish handwriting. But I did it, without disastrous consequences, and my mother got her trip to Israel.

I have never underestimated the amazing empowerment of this experience for me. In essence, my mother had entrusted me – aged eleven – with our family business. She had said: 'I believe in you, in your ability to do this'. And conversely, I have perhaps never fully estimated how demeaning this experience must have been for my father – what I gained, he lost.

***

I often regret that as an adult, I didn't engage with my father more. I realise now how little I knew about his family, and his background. Whatever I know, is only because my mother transmitted the information. He never, ever, spoke of his two sisters – whose existence remains an enigma to me. I used to think that he never spoke of them because he didn't want to. Perhaps it was simply that nobody asked.

My father died at the age of sixty-six. He had had routine surgery, and developed a deep vein thrombosis ten days later while he recuperated in hospital, lying resolutely in bed and refusing to comply with the nurses' demands that he get out of bed and move around.

I think he simply gave up.

CHAPTER 6.
THE EXTENDED FAMILY

My Parents with the extended Isaacson Family in South Africa, 1948

My father is staring, horrified, at the wall in our conventional, cluttered lounge. There is no sign of the usual hodgepodge of framed, familiar paintings that normally fill the space above the mantelpiece. Instead, there is a single painting — a tiny rectangular splash of abstract colour mounted at the very top of a large frame, the remainder of which is filled with blank white nothingness.

He yells at the top of his voice – 'Le-e-e-a, come quickly!! We have been robbed!!'

The perpetrator of the 'theft' – a very short, plump, elderly lady with thinning, strawberry blond hair in an asymmetric bob, sashays in with her arms folded across her ample bosom. 'Don't be dramatic, Samuel,' she admonishes. 'I simply replaced your usual poor taste with a nice, modern picture. It's high time you gave up your old Yiddish ways and moved into the modern South African era.'

My sister and I giggle nervously. Aunty Lily has arrived for her annual visit.

THE EXTENDED FAMILY

My grandmother, Rachel Charif (born Isaacson) was one of nine children. She was the eldest, with six brothers and two sisters. In the early 1900's her parents and all her siblings emigrated from Lithuania. She was the only one who remained behind. Two of the siblings emigrated to the USA, establishing the Isaacson family there. Her parents, (my great-grandparents) accompanied by six of their children – five sons and their youngest daughter, Lily – migrated to South Africa.

The South African branch of the Isaacson family lived in and around Dordrecht, a small rural town in the Eastern Cape. When my mother's brother, Hymie, left Lithuania in 1926, he went to join his grandparents and uncles there. Joseph, (the grandfather) died in December 1937, and Nachama (the grandmother) in 1940. They are both buried in the now dilapidated Jewish cemetery in Dordrecht, together with two of their sons and a daughter-in-law.

Lily, the youngest daughter, chose not to live with her parents and brothers in Dordrecht, instead heading to Johannesburg where she became fluent in English. She falsified her papers in order to change her date and country of birth, stating that she was born in South Africa. She studied nursing – but she suffered at the hands of the Matron who frequently criticised and denigrated her 'primitive ways'. As a consequence, she separated herself from her Yiddish influences, trying to re-invent herself as a modern, South African girl. This included the task of modernising and civilising her extended family – especially my mother, father, sister and me.

After she married, Lily and her husband Paul, and their son, Peter, settled in Pretoria, a town quite a distance from our hometown of Benoni. Paul was extremely tall, very austere and very Germanic. Lily – who stood less than 5 feet high – would look up at him lovingly, besotted with his stature. When he first met them, my father nicknamed Paul and Lily, behind their back, the *Vav* and the *Chirik* – two Hebrew vowels, one a long vertical stroke and the other the shortest apostrophe. Although being visibly mismatched, they were devoted to each other. Incredibly, they both died on the same day in 1972 – she after a long illness in hospital, and he after hearing the news of her death.

Lily didn't drive, so once or twice a year my mother would drive the two or three hours to Pretoria to fetch her, and bring her home for a visit. Each visit lasted a tumultuous week, at the end of which we always heaved a collective sigh of relief when my mom loaded her into the car to begin the return trip to Pretoria.

These visits by Aunty Lily continued regularly for much of our childhood, until she was too old, ill and frail to travel. Thereafter, and until Lily died, my mother would dutifully drive to Pretoria a few times a year to spend time with her. My mother simply overlooked all the drama Aunty Lily seemed to always introduce, and instead, loved and cared for her cantankerous aunt.

Being our grandmother's sister, Lily was granted the most amazing liberties in our home. She was allowed to riffle through our drawers, 'inspecting' them for neatness and passing judgment on my mother when things were not to her sterile, hospital standard. I once overheard her say some terrible, insulting things to my mother, who had been 'caught' sharpening a carving knife on a brick outside the kitchen. It may not have been the most sanitary thing to have done, but it was not deserving of the consequent tongue-lashing. Bewildered, I watched the tears rolling down my mother's cheeks, as she uncharacteristically said nothing. There was no rebuttal – Lily was her aunt, respect was obligatory, and so my mother simply accepted the unwarranted scolding.

My father, whose manners were a little rough around the edges, became the consummate gentleman when Aunty Lily was around. 'Please pass the *sault*' he would say, an exaggerated British accent layered over his thick Yiddish one, his baby finger delicately extended from the teacup handle. He tolerated her, as we all did, for my mother's sake.

Lily believed that she was the paragon of fashion – sporting the latest hairstyle, complete with thinly arched brows and red cupid lips. She frequently reminded us of her claim to fame – her apparent resemblance to the 1940's screen idol, Rita Hayworth.

She did as she pleased with us children – bullying us on the pretext of instilling 'modern values' into our lives. I remember her once putting a bowl over my sister's head and cutting her hair – badly – to emulate the latest 'layered' style she had seen in a magazine. Amazingly, my no-nonsense mother allowed it. She would excuse even the most outrageous behaviour, on the grounds that Aunty Lily really loved us, and everything she did was for our own good.

And on the rare occasion that my mother did protest, there would be tears and threats to phone for a taxi, always followed by my mother caving in to her demands and pleading with her to stay.

But despite the pretence of being a lady, (her own home was filled with the best German crockery, engraved silver cutlery and monogrammed linen), Aunty Lily had an Achilles heel of her own. On every visit to our home, she would sneak off to the corner cafe, where she would relish the hot potato chips, deep fried in a greasy fryer, loaded with salt and vinegar, and unhygienically wrapped in yesterday's newspaper. A far cry from the image of herself she sought to promote, but she simply could not resist.

***

Most families whose lives and possessions were destroyed during the Nazi regime have no mementos of their past. But because my mother's grandparents moved to South Africa before the Holocaust, we are fortunate to have letters, photographs and other meaningful and tangible connections to her past life. As a consequence, I have a collection of odd bits of furniture, each piece a physical memory of someone in the family.

When my mother arrived in South Africa, in July 1946, she met with her remaining three Isaacson uncles – Isaac, Julius and Saul. These three men became a close and integral part of our family. Although Uncle Isaac died when I was about four, he was somebody real – a grandfather substitute, of sorts – in my early childhood.

He had lost his wife, Sophie, to tuberculosis shortly after her arrival in Dordrecht, and had never remarried.

When my mother first met Isaac and Saul, they, and her brother, Hymie, were all living and working together on a farm in the Eastern Cape. After a short time, during which she noted that the men spent much of their day watching the clouds and waiting for rain, my mother convinced them to change lifestyles, and at her insistence, they all moved to small nearby towns and got jobs running stores and operating the local post offices. They all remained exceptionally close for the rest of their lives, even after Saul and Hymie found wives. In his later years, Uncle Isaac lived in a hotel in Brakpan, near to Hymie. I have in my dining room a small oak dresser that used to stand in his hotel bedroom, and opening it always evokes his memory – a warm, gentle, grandfatherly figure, with the Isaacson wishy-washy blue eyes, a ready smile, and a loving hug.

My mother's most prized possession was a beautiful brass *Samovar* – a traditional Russian urn used for making tea. It always stood at the centre of her dining table – in our family home in Benoni, her apartment in Johannesburg, and even half a world away, in her apartment, once she had migrated to Sydney, Australia. After my mother's death, the Samovar followed my sister to her home in Israel, and now lives with Eytan, my oldest nephew, in Sydney.

That Samovar is the closest thing we have to a family heirloom, and I remember my mother telling me how she came to own it.

It had belonged to my grandmother, Rachel. When Rachel's parents – Joseph and Nachama – had left for

South Africa, she had gifted it to them. When Nachama died, six years before my mother arrived in South Africa, the Samovar passed to Julius – the only married son at that time.

Fast forward a few years to when my mother, living in South Africa, went to visit her uncle Julius and his wife, Bella, in Johannesburg. Going to put something away in the pantry of their home, she noticed a brass item peeking out from beneath a dustcover, tucked away on a shelf. She immediately recognised it as her mother's Samovar, and overcome by emotion, fainted. When she finally came around and explained the enormity of her find, her aunt immediately gave it to her – in the process restoring to her a physical connection to her mother and 'home'.

I, too, have my own physical connection to the Isaacson family. My great-grandparents, Nachama and Joseph, had in their home, in Dordrecht, a heavy, square oak table with five solid carved legs. It once had the ability to expand to accommodate their large family in one sitting. I am not sure whether it accompanied them from Lithuania, or was bought in the Cape, but whatever its origins, it is old and precious.

For years that table stood humbly in the kitchen in our family home in Benoni, and it bears the scars from frequent use as an ironing board. But now it has pride of place in my lounge in Australia. I sometimes run my hands over its uneven surface, imagining the family gathered around it, hands resting on the wood, sharing a conversation, sharing a meal and I feel an indescribable sense of belonging.

THE EXTENDED FAMILY

***

My mother regarded the concept of family with great reverence, and she kept contact with everybody who fell under the umbrella of *Mishpocha* (family). This included family – close or distant – in South Africa, Israel and the United States (the offspring of Hyman and Rebecca, her mother's siblings), as well as many other far-flung corners of the world.

In South Africa, the family was extensive. There had been a large migration of Lithuanian Jews to South Africa at the end of the 19th Century, for both economic and religious reasons, and family from both my mother's and father's sides landed up living in South Africa.

In addition to her mother's family (the Isaacsons, as detailed above) there were offspring from my mother's father's siblings in South Africa too – the Burgins, the Charif's and the Krafchiks.

In the late 1800's in Russia, (and consequently Lithuania, which was intermittently ruled by Russia) most young men were conscripted into the Russian army. But if there was only one son in a family, that son was exempt from army service. It was thus common for some of the sons in Jewish families to adopt the surname of a maiden aunt, and thus, claiming to be an 'only son', escape being drafted. In this way, it turned out that my great grandfather, Mordechai Burgin had three sons, each with a different surname. The eldest, Joshua Burgin retained the family surname, the second, my grandfather, was Isaac Charif and the third son was Bernard Krafchik. I am not certain whether my grandfather's brothers migrated to South Africa, or remained in Lithuania, but most of their children and grandchildren lived in South Africa – mostly in the major cities, Johannesburg and Cape Town.

When she arrived in South Africa after the Holocaust, my mother connected with all of these relatives, from both sides of the family and ensured that we maintained regular contact with them. She was especially close to her cousin David Burgin (who was instrumental in her migration to South Africa), and his brother Ivan, with whom my family remained close friends until he died in the early 1970's.

My mother's father, in addition to his two brothers, also had two sisters – both of whom died in Lithuania before the Holocaust. Each sister had a daughter – Zelda Glickman, and Chaya Levitt. These young women had managed to survive the concentration camps and both lived in Israel. My mother had a special relationship with each of these first cousins, and spent time with them whenever she was in Israel. Zelda had other siblings. At least one brother, Morris, had migrated to South Africa, and my mother added him, and his children, and grandchildren, to the mishpocha list, too.

As well as maintaining a relationship with her own aunts, uncles and cousins – wherever she discovered them around the globe – my mother also kept in contact with the families of both my father, Samuel, and her first husband, Mokka.

She made my father's uncles and aunts and cousins her priority. My father's brothers and their children and grandchildren were closer to her than to him. Similarly,

THE EXTENDED FAMILY

she maintained a close relationship with Mokka's brother, Willy Klompus who lived in the Cape with his wife Ann and their two daughters, Hazel and Yvonne. I remember that when I was a child, my mother, sister and I spent regular holidays with them in their home in Camps Bay. They were seamlessly integrated with the rest of our extended family – as far as my mother was concerned, family was family, regardless of the path of connection.

Being so concerned with maintaining connection to the entirety of the extended family, it was also typical that my mother was the 'go to' person when someone in the family was in trouble.

A perfect example of this was Aunty Pere, my father's aunt – his father's sister. She had never married and had come via Ireland to Africa. My sister and I had never even heard of her until the day she arrived in our house – to live. It turns out Pere had been living on her own in Bulawayo, in what was then Rhodesia, (now Zimbabwe) and she had developed increasing dementia. She was found wandering the streets, in a state of mostly undress, and the authorities had found her connection to my mother via the regular cards and letters my mother had sent to her each year on *Rosh Hashana* (Jewish New Year). My mother dutifully travelled to Rhodesia, sorted out Pere's affairs and brought her back to our home where she lived for a couple of months, until the level of care she needed forced my mother to secure a place for this frail and demented soul in an old-aged home in Johannesburg. For the rest of Pere's life, there were obligatory visits to her there, which I absolutely hated, but 'she was family' and so we had no choice.

And this was far from a unique story – there were many other instances of relatives who would turn up and stay for a time while my mother tried to organise a better long-term option for them. My father used to say that she 'collected strays', bringing to our home aunts and uncles and cousins, no matter what the connection, as long as there was a family link. As a legacy from this behaviour, I have three mismatched antique chairs – each from one or another stray aunt whom my mother had temporarily rescued.

Before every Jewish New Year, for as long as she lived, my mother would sit at the dining room table, night after night, surrounded by greeting cards and familiar blue 'aerograms,' diligently writing to everyone in the family. She relished this ritual of greeting everyone individually and keeping the news from family members circulating around the globe, maintaining the connectedness and strengthening the family bonds. Doing this meant everything to her.

CHAPTER 7.
THE GRANDCHILDREN

*Top, left to right – Dan, Eytan; Middle,
left to right – Yaniv, David;
Bottom – Kerry; Australia, February 1992*

It is December 1991. We are all gathered around my mother's dining table in her apartment in Sydney. We have just arrived to live in Australia, and it is the first time in a long time that all the grandchildren are together in the one room. My mother is plying us with food. The small apartment is bursting with laughter and noise. There is music and joke-telling *and hugging and teasing happening all at once. I glance at my mother – her blue eyes are sparkling. She looks as if she will burst with love and joy.*

THE GRANDCHILDREN

As soon as her first grandchild was born, my mother became *Bobba* – the quintessential Jewish Grandmother. And as befits a Bobba, she plied her family and friends with copious food, memories and love

The title was used not only by her own grandchildren, but by everyone – her sons-in-law, my parents-in-law, all the children in the extended family, the students she tutored in her role as a Living Historian at the Jewish Day School – simply everyone knew her as Bobba.

My mother had five grandchildren – four grandsons and one granddaughter. The gift she gave to each of them was that they each believed they were her favourite. She had a knack of treating each of them differently – but equally.

She once explained to me that she didn't believe in the idea that because one child received something, the others should get the same. Each received what she perceived they needed – financial, material or emotional. She treated my sister and I in this way as well – equal but different. My mother believed, that in this way, everyone would have received the most from her, in the end.

I experienced this style of wisdom many times, but I most clearly recall it, when I first visited my sister in Australia in 1988. (My mother and I were still living in South Africa at that stage). My mother did not own a lot of 'good' jewellery, and had only one diamond ring – a modest solitaire engagement ring. She dealt with the potential problem of who would one day inherit the ring, in her unique way – choosing this visit of mine to Australia as the time to settle this issue. She gave me the ring and asked me to take it to give to my sister. She explained to me that I already had a solitaire engagement ring of my own, whereas my sister did not. (She had a ring with a band of multiple diamonds probably of equal or greater value – but my mother didn't see it in that way. The financial value was not the motivator.) By involving me in carrying out her decision, she made sure there was no room for misinterpretation of her wishes and no opportunity for jealousy or conflict, even if we were not being treated in the same way.

A few years later it was my turn to be the unequal recipient. When we first arrived in Australia, before we were financially secure, my son was offered a coveted place at a private school – but we were not in a position to pay the school fees. My mother stepped in, and paid the fees for the first year. This didn't set a precedent for the other grandchildren – it was simply her perception of our family need at the time.

I don't doubt that this style of giving was repeated amongst all of us, many, many times. It was simply her way – we were all 'unequally equal' – and we received according to need.

***

During my early married life, my parents and my sister and I, together with our respective families, all lived in South Africa, albeit in different cities.

My sister had migrated to Israel in 1969, and married there in 1970, but a few months after their first son, Eytan,

THE GRANDCHILDREN

was born in Jerusalem, the family returned to South Africa. They lived in Johannesburg. My family lived in Durban. My parents lived in Benoni. A few years after my father died, my mother moved to Johannesburg, initially living with my sister and her family in their home, and then moving to her own apartment.

Irrespective of where the grandchildren lived, my mother was a totally involved grandmother. Just before each grandchild was born, she would move into the home, and – asked or unasked – take over rearing the infant.

I vividly remember a story my sister told to illustrate this. A few weeks before Eytan – my mother's first grandchild – was born, my mother arrived in Israel 'to help'. She was there for the birth, and then remained for a few months, living with them in their tiny apartment in Jerusalem, and sharing a room with the baby. She insisted on doing the nightshift every night. And then insisted on doing the dayshift, too. As well as the cooking and shopping and house-keeping. So soon she was exhausted, but she refused to give up any of her self-assigned roles.

My sister hatched a plan to give my mother an undisturbed night. When my mother – and the baby – were asleep, she crept into the room, stole her sleeping baby in his crib and brought him to her own room for the night. When she awoke in the morning, amazed at how well the baby had slept, she discovered him missing.

He was, of course, back with my mother. She had woken in the night, found the baby missing, crept into my sister's room and stolen him back!

Each subsequent baby was treated in the same way. My

mother would move in and take over. She was no different in her desire to take over when my children were born, although I was a little more successful in my resistance.

When my first child was born, my husband had six weeks leave from Border Duty in the South African army, to which he had been conscripted. My mother duly arrived to 'help with the baby' and was ready to settle in for the long haul, to keep me company when my husband went back to the army.

She was a little taken aback when, after five weeks, I told her it was time for her to go home. She refused at first – but eventually we negotiated a settlement when I agreed to employ somebody to help me in her stead. (That somebody turned out to be Lucy – a young domestic worker who started as a cleaner in my home and soon became my trusted nanny, and my children's second mother for twelve years, until the day we left South Africa to migrate to Australia.)

By the time my second child was born – Bobba's last grandchild – she had come around to accepting that 'help' was a finite quality.

As babies, the grandchildren all got more or less the same amount of time with Bobba. She would have been happy to take full control over every aspect of their lives during their first year, had my sister and I permitted it. But when the children got older, the amount of time they spent with their Bobba was different.

My sister's children got Bobba's day-to-day involvement. She was a constant in their lives – there for every school function, every Shabbat, every occasion. She was always there as back-up – when my sister worked or went on holiday. She was the one who was around, to rush them to the doctor when Dan accidentally swallowed paraffin, or mangled his finger; or Eytan burnt his leg when he pulled over a pot of boiling water; or any of the other myriad disasters that befell the boys as a consequence of being, simply, boys.

By contrast, my children got 'feast and famine' grandparenting, with Bobba's full attention two or three times a year, when she would visit us in Durban for an extended period – often over the children's birthdays or for Jewish festivals. She would cook and bake, preparing all the family's favourite foods, swim and garden and spend every moment of every day involved in our lives. She taught the children to play *Scrabble* (albeit with her odd Yiddish-phonetic spelling) and *Rummicub*, which we played every night as our favourite ritual. And then she would go back home, and there would be a void, until the next visit.

When we moved to Australia, the pattern repeated – our family lived in Brisbane, my mother and the other grandchildren lived in Sydney.

One would expect that these two styles of grandparenting would lead to different relationships with her grandchildren – but the bond she had with each of them was fundamentally the same. In her own way, each received an equal but different measure of her unconditional love, pride, precious stories, and of course, copious amounts of food!

PART TWO:
FRIENDSHIP

My mother is telling us stories from 'home'. Her favourite is about Yosele - a naive young boy in her class who always sought favour with the older boys. Gleefully offering to hide an egg under his hat, he sets himself up to be the brunt of their prank. When one of the older boys claps him on the head in greeting, Yosele is left, literally, with egg on his face.

As she tells the silly story for the umpteenth time, choking back laughter, tears of mirth run down my mother's face. Then the tears change to torrents of sadness, as she recalls that almost everyone from that time has been killed.

Her tales of friendship from those days are always bittersweet.

CHAPTER 8.
EARLY FRIENDSHIPS

(LITHUANIA, 1914-1943)

My mother was naturally gregarious. She made friends easily and she retained many of her friends for life. We often joked that even if she had landed in the middle of Siberia, within a short time she would have been surrounded by friends. She saw the good and the potential in all people – her natural optimism generally finding a positive aspect in everyone. She easily endeared herself to people, and a lot of her friends were simply in awe of her.

She was also a natural leader – constantly organising others for the good of the group. She was fair and principled, but she didn't suffer fools gladly, and she expected the unwavering loyalty she gave to her friends to be reciprocated.

It was during my mother's incarceration in the concentration camps that loyalty and friendship really came to the fore. My mother's natural leadership qualities stood her in good stead. She was brave and she was smart and she went out on a limb for others. In return, they took risks for her.

Stories of her youth and early student days were often

centred around one or other group of young friends – from the classes she attended, or the youth groups, or the natural activities the environment lent itself to – outings, dances, and ice skating. Stories from those days were packed with frivolity and the joy of relative privilege – attending high-school functions and social activities at university; tales of girlfriends and boyfriends abound.

Even after she married Mokka and became a mother, the friendships continued. She told many stories about her and her friends attending charity balls together, or going out to shows and restaurants during the heady days of the late 1920's and early 1930's. It sounded like a fun time.

But it all ended with the German invasion of Lithuania.

My mother had a photograph of her final high-school class hanging on her wall. She would point out all of her friends, and teachers, and then, one by one, describe their collective fate. Of the entire group, only four of the students – the few lucky ones – survived. All of the others – either living in Kovno, or Vilna, or Wilkomir, or any of the surrounding towns – had been rounded up and killed in the concentration camps.

One of the surviving classmates was Nadia. She and my mother finished high-school together, and they were at university together. Nadia married a Frenchman, Henri, in 1933 and moved to Paris before the war. During the German occupation she went into hiding in the Pyrenees mountains. Nadia's husband, too, was a survivor – after they married, he served in the French army, and got captured. He was later freed in exchange for a German general; thus he, too, remained in hiding until liberation.

They had an apartment in Paris, but their main home and business was in the French countryside. While they were in hiding, their French neighbours maintained the home and business, and when they returned after the war ended, it was all given back to them, so they were able to quickly return to relatively 'normal' life in Paris.

After her liberation from Bergen-Belsen, my mother and Nadia reconnected through an organisation in which volunteers tried to connect and repatriate survivors of the Holocaust. En route to South Africa, my mother spent four months living with Nadia and her husband, Henri, in their home in Paris.

I remember when Nadia came to visit us in South Africa many years later. She was quintessentially French — chic, beautifully made up, her hair in a chignon, and wearing a designer pants suit.

She told me how, during that visit to Paris, my mother had slept in bed with her, curled up like a child between her and her husband, and how together they nursed her through the horrendous nightmares she suffered night after night. Nadia explained they were so concerned about my mother's mental health that they took turns to stay home with her, never leaving her alone.

My mother insisted that her childhood friend had saved her life. She often said that were it not for the amazing love and care that she received from Nadia and Henri at that time, she might well have survived the concentration camps, only to have died in the aftermath.

CHAPTER 9.
FRIENDS IN THE CAMPS

(ESTONIA AND GERMANY, 1943–1945)

My mother and her 'daughters' from the camps, taken at Bergen-Belsen after liberation. 1946.

My mother is wrapped in a threadbare grey blanket, lying on the ground in thick snow. She is weak from typhus, and unable to stand. Together with all the inmates from the 'hospital' she has been pushed outside, into the cold, and left to die.

Suddenly, two of her friends appear. At great personal risk, they have come to look for her, bringing clothes to dress her in. They clothe her, lift her up, and, carrying her between them, drag her to the place where the rest of the camp has been assembled for transfer to a new location. They slip her into the line with the healthy inmates, supporting her as they march in groups of ten, towards the train.

One of her friends – a nurse – pushes her unseen into a train carriage filled with medical equipment, and locks her in. Against all odds, she survives.

***

As soon as she arrived at the first concentration camp in Estonia – Vaivara – my mother was put to work. Like many of the women, she was assigned to a team of four, to stand day after day, knee deep in snow, wearing a skimpy dress and ill-fitting clogs, tasked with cutting down enormous trees. It was dangerous work, and there were many injuries. They had only rudimentary equipment and no skill, and they were freezing.

After two weeks, the *Lager Fuhrer* gathered some of the women, including my mother, on the *appelplatz*. She recalls that she was quite happy that she had been selected – she assumed he was sending them to Auschwitz, to be killed – as she would not have to go to work in the woods anymore. But she was wrong. Instead of being selected as part of a group transport, he selected her instead to be in charge of the women's barrack at the camp.

> The block contained three big rooms, each housing one hundred women, with bunks around the walls. Each bunk was one meter wide and was shared by five women. Each bunk had straw and a single blanket. We were like sardines. When we had to turn, we all had to turn – one could not turn alone – there wasn't enough room.

The barracks were locked from outside at night, and there were no toilet facilities. Living in such close proximity, and with the terrible food they were given, the women all got diarrhea. They used the buckets that the food arrived in as toilets, and my mother's job was to clean the buckets, and the inevitable overflow, and keep the barrack in order.

> It had to be clean and done, because the inspection is coming. The people are all away on work, and the inspection is coming. And the straw had to be straightened, and the blanket has to be straightened and everything has to be all precisely arranged. It was very hard work; it was terrible work – but I was happier – I wasn't bleeding from injuries from the trees – and my wounds could heal.

My mother was a hard worker, but the work assigned to her in the barracks was more than any one person could do. Undaunted, she approached the *Lager Fuhrer* and, speaking in fluent German, convinced him that she needed help. He arranged it.

As part of their hierarchy in controlling the inmates, the Nazis recruited *Kappos* – Jews who acted as police and henchmen, carrying out the work of the SS. The *Kappo* at Vaivara was a hated, Jewish Polish man, who collected the women for work every day, often beating them when they did not comply. My mother couldn't stand the unnecessary brutality, and set about getting him onside.

> We were one hundred in there, some old ladies and young girls and sick ones. When he used to come in with a big stick like that, he used to come in and hit them over the shoulder when they didn't want to go

out to work. He needed about 60 or 65 women and sometimes he really used to break their bones. So I once said to him, I said 'listen, don't come in to hit them. Tell me how many you need and I will make a list and I will give you the 65 you need, or the 60 – just come and tell me in the evening that you need so many people tomorrow morning and I will have them ready for you'. He had a little pencil – he couldn't write, I am sure he couldn't write – but he had a little pencil. And I said, 'give it to me'. He said 'here – if you are so educated, you write the names'. So I did.

My mother gathered all the women in the barrack and proposed a roster system, which she managed.

Let us send to work the healthy ones, the young ones. I promise you that after you work a few days you'll have a rest – I'll swap you. We'll leave the old people with the young girls, let them stay in the barracks and not go to work. And they agreed to it. They listened to me. And I had a list and I had every night my 65 women and that was fine. Every day I used to go out and bring my 65 to the *Kappo*, and the *Lager Fuhrer* saw it. He saw that in my camp, everything is orderly.

Inadvertently, she gained the camp leader's grudging respect. More importantly, she gained the love and respect of the women in the barracks, for whom life had become a little more bearable. The people who remained in the barrack each day helped with the cleaning, and she established a relationship with the kitchen staff, enabling her access to coal and wood, so that the barrack was a little warmer when the women returned from working, and there was hot water to drink. Step by step, she succeeded in taking some control of an untenable situation, and making it a little better for everyone.

Early on in the camps, my mother recognised the importance of connectedness. She instinctively knew that friendship and belonging helped to overcome the dehumanisation the Nazis sought to perpetrate. During her time in the camps, she gathered around her a group of about ten younger women who became her friends. She talked of them as *her girls* or *her adopted daughters* – the reference to family speaking volumes of the nature of their relationship. They looked out for each other. They made sacrifices for each other. And, they survived together.

> We were mostly from Kovno, from Lithuania our group. We were all the time like a whole group, we always were standing together, and this helped us a lot because we could utilise a little bit of our mental exercises. We came from one place so we had the same schooling, we had the Hebrew language all of us and whenever we had a chance, we were just sitting and telling each other stories, stories about what we had studied or stories from home – trying not to forget who and what we are.

One of *her girls* – a teenager – was smaller and frailer than the others, and struggled to make it through the 24 hours between one meagre meal and the next. As the day wore on, she would faint from hunger, putting herself at risk of deportation if this was ever observed by the *Blitzwomen* or another Nazi official. My mother made a plan to save her. She gathered the others and arranged for each of them to retain a little of their daily ration of bread, in order to give it to the girl during the course of the day and prevent her from fainting. For women who received watery soup and just one tenth of a loaf of bread as their only sustenance each day, it was a huge sacrifice. But my mother asked it of them, and they all complied.

***

A short while after she took over running the women's barrack, my mother became ill with typhus. The *Lager Fuhrer* did not order her to be sent to Auschwitz (which was the usual fate of someone who could no longer pull their weight), but personally ordered she be taken to the camp's medical facility to recover. Although there was no real medical help, a Jewish doctor was allowed to visit daily.

> The doctor also came with us, [to Vaivara] from Kovno. Dr Kamba was her name. She was an old lady. She was coming in – there was no medicine, no food, nothing – we were just lying there. But one day she came with a big pumpkin, and was standing there with a knife and

dividing it into 60 small little pieces, and our eyes were just standing out – they were looking, looking for this piece of pumpkin that she was going to give us. That piece of pumpkin – that was our food that we had, and that was our medicine.

Despite it being forbidden, two of her friends would also visit my mother in the medical facility. Dora, one of her girls, was a nurse who worked with Dr Kamba. The other, Miryam was only an occasional member of the group, but she adored my mother. Miryam had been chosen as an involuntary 'companion' to the Nazi leader of the *Blitzwomen*, with whom she was forced to sleep. This role provided her some additional liberties, and she used her 'privileged position' to visit my mother, taking her food when she could, and keeping an eye out for her.

Eventually, my mother was on the road to recovery. But before she was well enough to leave the medical facility, the camp was closed to avoid the approaching Russian army. The staff and occupants were ordered to move to a new camp, and the patients in the medical facility were wrapped in their thin blankets and thrown outside onto the snow, and left to die.

It was her friends – Dora and Miryam – who came to find her. These were the friends who dressed her and supported her and pushed her onto the train bound for the new camp, locking her into a carriage filled with equipment from the medical facility. These were her friends who ensured that she survived.

> The Germans were busy outside the train and didn't notice, and she – Dora – just pushed me in and locked me up in that carriage. And we were taken from there to another camp, called Erida.

***

This pattern of camp closures and transfers happened repeatedly – as the Russian army approached, the inmates were moved to a different camp. In total, my mother spent time in five camps. Each time, as part of the transfer process, there were also *selektions* during which weak and infirm people were removed and sent for extermination.

The core group of *her girls* remained together in most of the camps. When they were transferred to Stutthof, a staging point between Erida and the next concentration camp, two more women joined the group. The first was my mother's first cousin, who had been brought to Stutthof after surviving death in another camp by hiding in the ceiling. During the 'sorting process' at Stutthof, this cousin was selected to remain alive. The second was a child – a young girl who, on arrival in Stutthof, had already (together with Dr Kamba – their Kovno doctor) been selected for extermination.

> They were left there outside the barracks, to be sent away. So we, the Kovno girls, got together. First of all,

that's our doctor Kamba there, and secondly, they knew that little girl, some of them knew her. What were we going to do about it? A Russian lady (she was a prostitute) was in charge of watching them – she was looking after them. We still had something hidden – a chain, a watch, some money, someone had a ring – so we decided to put together a parcel. I approached this woman (I could speak Russian) and I told her what we would give her if she would take out these two women for us. And she did. She brought me that little girl, and the doctor, Dr Kamba, and I gave her what I have for her. We took them back to the barrack where we were. The next morning, Dr Kamba was dead. She had committed suicide that night, knowing that, with her grey hair, tomorrow they would take her back. But the little girl – Chayale, (she wasn't so little, she was 14, but she looked like 10) – she remained with me, and became my adopted daughter.

Chayale stayed with my mother throughout the remainder of the camps. They were together in Ochsenzoll, and they survived Bergen-Belsen together. They remained together after the war in the displaced person's camp, and only separated when my mother went to South Africa, and she to Israel. They were reunited when my mother visited Israel some years later.

In 1970 in Israel, at my sister's wedding, a group of women came to celebrate with my mother. They were *her girls*. The photograph of them together, in happy circumstances some 25 years after liberation, bears testament to the depth of their relationship. That photograph had pride of place alongside a small notebook that was one of my mother's most precious possessions. The book – the cover, pages and inscriptions – was handmade by *her girls*, using scraps of a Canadian soldier's uniform, and presented to her on her birthday, the day before she left Bergen-Belsen.

Although the photograph and the book have become faded with age, both illustrate in a tangible way this incredible group friendship that was forged in the most difficult of circumstances, and which, despite years and distance, never lost its lustre.

CHAPTER 10.
FRIENDS AND LIBERATION

(GERMANY, EUROPE, 1945-1946)

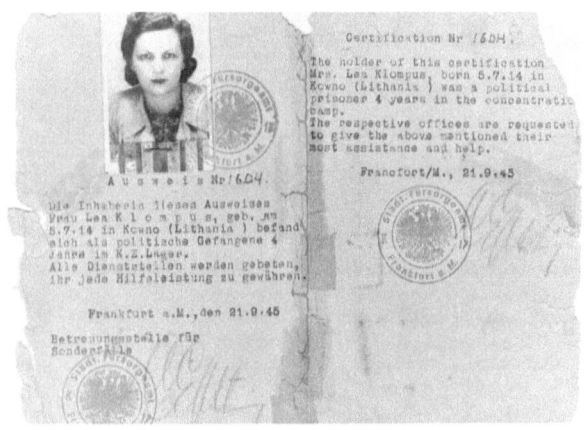

*My mother's certificate identifying her as
a concentration camp survivor, Frankfurt. 1945*

Miriam is shouting excitedly into the phone. 'She's alive' she yells. 'Hymie – she's alive!! Layke is alive. I've just seen her on the newsreel – the one showing survivors from Bergen-Belsen. Hymie – I'd know her anywhere – she was my close friend. Can you believe? She's alive!!'

NOT JUST A SURVIVOR

After liberation, a whole new adjustment period began. The immediate trauma of starvation and deprivation was over, but the road to recovery was a long and tortuous one that each survivor traversed, many unsuccessfully.

The adjustment began by trying to connect with loved ones – and discovering, for many, that almost all of those loved ones were gone. There were the practical problems of where to go, and what to do. How to pick up the pieces of a life that had been shattered into so many fragments; all its primary connections severed. There was the realisation of what had actually happened, and, in the face of so much death, a sense of guilt for surviving, was ever present.

The reality of the physical and psychological trauma of the concentration camps, and of survival, was almost insurmountable, and, for survivors – as well as many of the members of the Allied forces who liberated them – the impact was life-long.

> We were unexpectedly free. We had survived! We were reborn a second time. Orphans, alone in a strange world. We had to learn to fit into a new society, to adapt to a strange way of life. Though our *self* which we had preserved from the first world was still with us, it had been in a static state for four years, and although it did not regress, it didn't progress either. We lacked much of the refinement that the rest of society's progress had created. We tried extremely hard to pick up the broken threads of our lives, we adjusted to the demands of the various new environments and new ways of life,

> but we could never be like you. And you could never understand us. We are different and our inner world is different. We are forever burdened by personal, horrendous memories that are continually recalled to mind, and they in turn influence and direct our behaviour and our sense of self. This abnormal is our normal. And it never goes away.

In the light of this, it made sense that almost all the relationships my mother had for the rest of her life, shared the commonality of the Holocaust. All her friends had either lived in Lithuania before the war or were Holocaust survivors in one form or another. Although she had acquaintances from other walks of life, they were always peripheral, always foreigners.

In the immediate aftermath of the war, my mother lived and worked in Bergen-Belsen – which, after liberation, was 'converted' into a displaced person's camp run by the Allies. She was there for about a year. During that time, the camaraderie of *her girls* sustained her. They shared a history that didn't require explanation. They shared the same problems, and they were each part of the other's solution. But she also needed to move forward towards creating a new life.

As soon as Bergen-Belsen was liberated, in April 1945, my mother collapsed and spent three weeks in hospital in a semi-conscious state. After she recovered, she began working for the newly installed Commanding Officer of Bergen-Belsen. He treated her like an equal. She shared his office, and was paid for her work. He taught her, and her friends, conversational English. He ensured she had extra rations and cigarettes and she ate in the officer's mess. She felt valued and she felt human. His kindness to her was probably the first part of her rehabilitation towards normality.

This experience gave her enough confidence to challenge a replacement Commanding Officer of Bergen-Belsen, who arrived several months later and who tried to treat her as an inferior.

From the moment the new Commanding Officer arrived, there was friction. The outgoing Commanding Officer introduced them, and the new man refused to shake her hand. Then he moved her desk out to a separate room, and he wouldn't allow her access to certain documents. He told the Allied staff in the camp that the Jewish survivors were Russian spies and were thus not to be trusted with anything important. She had soon had enough.

> I told him: 'I am working here. I am not forced to work here – the Germans forced me enough – but now it's my own goodwill that I'm working for you. If you are not going to treat me like an equal to you, like an equal human being, then I am not going to work for you'. So I said goodbye, and I went away.

During that time, my mother had another agenda. She needed to establish whether her husband, Mokka, was still alive. So she joined the *Bricha* representatives who came to Bergen-Belsen, trying to recruit illegal immigrants to Israel. She was fluent in Hebrew, German, Russian, Lithuanian and Yiddish and spoke English quite well, so they readily accepted her offer to join them. She travelled with them throughout Europe – through many countries and many abandoned camps – looking for survivors who were in hiding. She went to Prague and Budapest and Vienna and Munich, and many other cities, and brought many survivors back to Bergen-Belsen.

But she didn't find her husband.

> I couldn't find any trace of him. Nowhere. Not where he was in the camps, not where he was killed, nothing at all. I couldn't find anything – any lists or any names. I didn't hear anything about him. And I didn't know for many, many years. I don't know, even now. But I heard, many years later, that 500 people who were in Stutthof at the time, just before liberation, were put onto boats – they were telling them they were going to Hamburg or something – but they took them to sea and killed them. I think he might have been one of them. But I don't know for sure.

***

Before the connection had been made, between my mother, in the Bergen-Belsen displaced person's camp, and Hymie, her brother in South Africa, nobody outside of

Bergen-Belsen knew whether or not she was alive.

During that time, newsreels of the war were being screened in every movie theatre, as a prelude to the main feature film. Mickey – her school friend who had immigrated to South Africa before the war – was watching a newsreel showing the liberated inmates from Bergen-Belsen and became convinced she had seen my mother in the newsreel. She was so excited that she didn't stay to watch the main feature but ran out of the theatre immediately to contact Hymie – shouting that she had seen Lea in the film and was sure she was alive.

My mother and Mickey were re-united when my mother got to South Africa. Our families eventually lived in the same small town, around the corner from each other, and she and Mickey remained friends until Mickey died.

***

Finally, she had her emigration papers.

My mother was the first survivor to arrive in South Africa – albeit on a visitor's visa, as South Africa was not accepting Jewish Holocaust survivors at the time. Because of the visa requirement, she spent some time in Lisbon, Portugal, prior to boarding a boat there for Lourenco Marques – the capital of Mozambique, at the time a Portuguese colony, (now Maputo).

On her first Shabbat in Lisbon, alone and in a very fragile state, she decided to attend the synagogue service. She went there looking for familiarity and comfort. Instead, she found isolation. The tight-knit circle of women was cold and alienating, and she felt that they were judging her, staring and pointing. She stumbled out of the building sobbing, and began running back to her hotel. Lost and disorientated, she realised somebody was following her.

Her name was Mariana Pereira Correia, and she was a Catholic nun. She reached out to my mother, offering compassion and companionship. For the duration of my mother's stay in Lisbon, Mariana would collect her at the hotel every morning and spend the entire day with her. She would show her the sights of the city, discuss history and geography and art with her, and ensure that she was not alone for any length of time. The day that the ship sailed, she was there to wave my mother goodbye. She had thoughtfully brought a gift for the journey – a simple striped *Cadera* (deckchair) – so that my mother would be able to enjoy the ship's deck in comfort.

I found among my mother's papers a small deck of photographs of Lisbon, with English commentary in beautiful, neat handwriting, detailing where they had been, and what they had spoken of. The farewell greeting ended hoping they would meet again in Portugal in the future.

CHAPTER 11.
FRIENDS IN A NEW WORLD

(SOUTH AFRICA AND AUSTRALIA, 1946–2000)

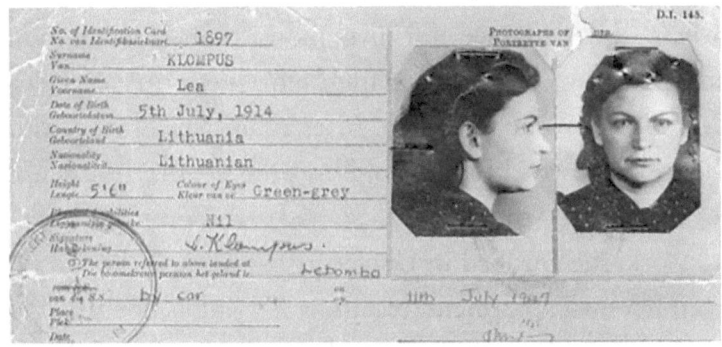

South African Identity Document, 1947

My mother's initial time in South Africa was traumatic. She received incredible financial and emotional support from her brother and cousins and extended family, but she was physically and mentally ill. A vicious kick from a Nazi boot in the last days before liberation had fractured a vertebra in her lower back, and when she was safely ensconced in family care, the accumulated emotional, somatic and psychiatric trauma finally amalgamated and presented as total paralysis from her waist down.

She was admitted to Johannesburg General Hospital where she remained for five months of rehabilitation and therapy, before regaining movement in her legs. Miraculously, she recovered. After a short spell living with her cousin, David Burgin, and his wife, Roche, the essence of my mother – the survivor – started to reappear. She began to work, she enrolled in University studies and she moved into her own apartment, regaining her independence.

From the time that my mother arrived in South Africa in 1946 until the day she left for Australia in 1990, she befriended every Holocaust survivor that she ever met. Her social and communal life were intertwined – centred around people who had experienced the Holocaust, who shared her Lithuanian origin, or who were Holocaust survivors from a different country. She considered them all to be her friends, all to be her family.

She was a founder member of the Malater Society, an organisation established for those who came from Malat, her hometown in Lithuania. Anyone who had originated from her hometown or the surrounding towns had automatic access to her support, and unwavering loyalty

– despite their individual personalities, social standing or education. It made for some strange friendships, and I recall them all – a motley group of displaced, for the most part disturbed, men and women, each in their own ways trying desperately to be 'normal' and fit into a society that failed to empathise with their differences and trauma.

***

There was one special friend, however, who had no Holocaust connection. This unlikely and unintended 'best' friend was a small black and white fox-terrier – a companion that filled a void in her life that nobody else seemed capable of. His name was Kelly.

He arrived in our family as an eight-week-old puppy, when I was two, and was supposed to be for my sister and me. But in a short time, he attached himself to my mother and forever after was her self-appointed companion and guardian. At night, he slept at her feet as she studied at the dining room table. If a stranger approached her, he positioned himself between them – one step too close and he bared his teeth.

Wherever she went, he followed. She would pick up her car keys and tell him where she was headed and he somehow knew that when she went to Johannesburg – or to work during regular hours – he couldn't go with her. But everywhere else, he was her shadow. He would escape the locked house and arrive upstairs at the synagogue, locate her seat and lie quietly underneath it. He could find her car parked in the main street in the town centre, and be lying watchfully on the pavement next to it, waiting for her to emerge from the shops. If he did accompany her to the department stores, he would run up the stairs, and be waiting at the next floor for her as the lift door opened. If he was left in the car, and the parcels of meat next to him became too tempting, he would move to the front seat to avoid them.

If she ever needed to go to The Shop after hours, Kelly went with her. Once, he was unwittingly left behind there, and when my mother realised he was missing and went back to look for him some hours later, he had already run ten of the sixteen miles home along the highway. His paw pads were rubbed raw, but he fully intended to find his way back to her.

He was by far the smartest and most loyal dog I have ever met.

When he was twelve years old, Kelly got into a dog fight, and was so badly injured that he couldn't be saved. After twelve years of total companionship, he was gone, and my mother was bereft.

I seldom saw my mother cry. When she lit a *Yahrzeit* (annual memorial) candle for her family, or when we went to *Yom HaShoah* (Day of Remembrance) services, she would bow her head, and a tear would roll down her cheek, or her eyes would glisten with unshed tears. But for the most part, when she told her Holocaust story, she was quite stoic. Yet, for weeks after Kelly died, my mother would cry uncontrollably every time she picked up her car keys. She once admitted to me – with amazement and some degree of shame – that she couldn't understand how she could cry for the loss of this little dog after all the human loss and suffering she had endured. But he had wheedled his way into her heart, and it was many years before she stopped mourning him.

***

My mother lived in South Africa for almost 45 years, but it was never 'home' for her in the way Lithuania had been. In South Africa she had married, had children, studied, worked, and had friends, but she never felt as if she truly belonged. Initially, it was going to be an interim stop on the way to her long-term plans to migrate to Israel. But as time went on, she established a family and new obligations, and remained tethered to South Africa.

In 1986, my sister and her family migrated to Sydney, Australia and my mother wanted to join them. She firmly believed the political situation in South Africa was deteriorating rapidly and she didn't want to be part of yet another country's descent into turmoil. She also thought that if *she* migrated it might hasten and facilitate my decision to follow.

Her emigration to Australia in 1990 had its own challenges. She was leaving her elderly brother, Hymie, behind. She was severing all the ties she had spent a lifetime re-creating after her Holocaust experiences. And she faced starting again at an advanced age in relatively poor health, on another continent.

For a number of reasons, she chose to travel to Australia by ship. She wanted the time on the seas to make the emotional transition. She had arrived in South Africa by boat and she felt she should leave the same way. She had ongoing problems with her back, and thought the ship experience would be more comfortable than a long flight. And – the deal-clincher – she could carry much more luggage on the boat than a plane would allow. So she booked her passage on the *Achilles Lauro*, and six weeks later, she docked in Sydney.

My sister and brother-in-law were waiting for her, and in her usual style, paying no attention to protocol, my mother simply walked off the boat. She had by-passed the customs and disembarkation procedure, and had no luggage with her. By the time the family had dragged her back to complete the formalities, her luggage had been sent to a storage facility, and could only be collected after midday. So they all waited around, and at the appointed time, they went to pick her suitcase up. As they approached the baggage shed, they heard a loud siren. My sister said that, as it was midday, she thought it was to signal a change of shift. But the siren continued wailing, and as they approached, it got louder and louder. The wailing was clearly emanating from a suitcase that was standing alone and had been cordoned off.

Of course, it belonged to my mother.

As she rushed to grab it, she found herself instantly surrounded by security guards, and a crowd of curious onlookers. After some discussion, she managed to convince them that the suitcase was innocuous, although she, too, was baffled by the sound. When they warily allowed her to open the suitcase, she broke into a broad grin of recognition – the blaring siren was on one end of a very large, very heavy torch she had in her suitcase, that must have accidentally turned on while her suitcase was being bumped around in the disembarkation process.

She then explained to the bemused crowd that, despite the heavy torch also being a potential weapon, she would only ever have used it as such, if she was alone in The Shop and she had needed to cosh someone over the head with it. The siren would have sounded and frightened the offender off. She added disarmingly that, now she was in Australia, she was sure she wouldn't need to use it, other than as a warning.

My mother had arrived.

In Australia, as she had first done in South Africa 45 years earlier, she quickly set about joining the Holocaust survivors' network, building friendships and garnering support. Within a few months, she had re-established herself. At the tender age of 76, she threw herself headlong into a new country, a new home, and new connections. She soon became friends with a diverse group of people of all ages. Among them were survivors from her past, with whom she reconnected, members of the ex-South African Jewish community, and Australian Holocaust survivors. Building on these relationships, she became a volunteer tour guide at the Sydney Holocaust Museum and a 'Living Historian' at Masada college (one of Sydney's large Jewish day-schools).

Among the friends who lived close by, she established a regular *Rummicub* group. They played together every night at her apartment, and she baked and cooked for them to her heart's content. She lived in an area in the Eastern

Suburbs of Sydney, with numerous food stores and delis literally outside her door, and she could afford to shop there if she chose. But she liked a bargain, didn't believe in wasting, and delighted in 'beating the system', if she could.

She discovered a discount food market quite a distance away from her home, that sold produce at reduced prices. The bus and rail system in Sydney at the time charged pensioners one dollar a day for unlimited travel. So she would hop on the bus to 'her market', buy what she could carry, go home by bus, offload and repeat this as many times as she needed to do her shopping. Despite my sister's protests at this practice, my mother was adamant – the transport was almost free, she had the time, and 'why waste if there is a perfect alternative'?

My mother might have been frugal for herself, but she was always generous to others. She donated to every Jewish charity that asked, to every beggar that put a hand out, and to most charities that involved dogs. She believed if someone asked for help, she was obliged to give it. Material things meant nothing to her. If you admired something of hers, she would willingly give it to you. She would literally give you the shirt off her back if she thought you needed it.

Before long, she decided that the *Rummicub* group should all contribute a nominal amount – a negligible 'entry-fee' of sorts – which she would donate to charity on their collective behalf.

One of the members of the group – an elderly gentleman, also a Holocaust survivor, who lived in the same building a few floors below my mother – objected. He had a car and did most of the transporting of the elderly ladies to and from each meeting, and thought it unfair that he should pay for petrol, and still have to contribute to charity. He was unceremoniously dumped from the group. Incensed by his meanness, my mother pointed out that she was paying for the food they consumed which more than offset the cost of his petrol.

Over time, their frosty relationship repaired a little – they both lived in the same building, so they continued to bump into each other. But despite eventually back-pedalling on the charity issue, he was never invited back into the *Rummicub* group, because she never forgot that he was uncharitable and mean-spirited. Those qualities were, to her, unforgivable.

My mother lived happily in Sydney for close to ten years. She simply transferred countries, taking her history, her belief system and her Holocaust connectivity along with her. But, as with South Africa, Australia was never home. 'Home' remained Malat and Kovno in Lithuania, and when she became ill, just before she died, she stopped speaking English and Hebrew, and reverted first to Yiddish, and finally, to something unintelligible, which we assumed was most likely Lithuanian or Russian.

In her mind, she simply went back 'home'.

PART THREE:
FOOD

In the many years since my mother has died, her voice has not been silenced. I hear her opinions, her criticisms, her accolades. I see her nodding approval as the fragrant challah I am baking comes out of the oven, or frowning as my taiglach collapse, failing to emulate hers. Her words, her ways, are ingrained in my subconscious as if she were right beside me in so many aspects of my life, but most especially, in my kitchen.

Long before it became politically correct to do so, my mother was a recycler. The commodity she recycled was not plastic, or paper, or glass (although she certainly hoarded and reused all of these) – but food.

I never, ever, saw her throw away food. Despite the availability of abundant food during my lifetime, not a single morsel was ever wasted. Vegetable peels became soup. Citrus peels became candy. An unsuccessful cake was eaten anyway, or at very worst, grated and dried and re-purposed as biscuit crumbs. Leftovers in the fridge were minced and reappeared as *perogen* (small meat pies served in soup), sour milk was transformed into cheese and oil was strained and reused again and again until every last drop was consumed.

Food, for my mother, was treated as the most precious resource on earth. And, for the years of her incarceration in Nazi camps, it was.

Her story, from the Kovno Ghetto to living in freedom in South Africa, is punctuated at every turn with references to food: crusts of bread became her bargaining tools, a piece of turnip her medicine, a scrap of pumpkin her saviour.

CHAPTER 12.
MY MOTHER AND FOOD

Food was my mother's connection to Malat – the place where she lived for less than a quarter of her life, but which was forever designated 'home'. Her love of cooking and baking came from her mother. Her parents had owned a restaurant and bakery there, and the traditional foods she made in her mother's memory, were tangible and evocative reminders of a happy time and place, long gone.

As a child, while my mother worked and studied, she handed over the day-to-day cooking to our very capable domestic helper. But on most Sunday mornings, and before every Jewish festival, she would resume full control of the kitchen which she would fill with fragrant and beautiful delicacies, that transported us all to Malat.

I especially remember watching my mother prepare for the Jewish festivals. She would describe how she would come home for the school holidays and help her parents bake *matzo* for the entire small village – preparing and baking the dough in the prescribed way to avoid fermenting and rising. Her eyes would glisten as she would recall the white tablecloth of her mother's kitchen, the endless array of festive foods they would make – *gefilte fish* and myriad forms of herring, *kneidlach* and chicken soup, light-as-a-feather flourless sponge cakes and crispy, syrup-coated *taiglach*. And then, a world apart, she would recreate in our family kitchen the same feast, linking with food our past, present and future.

***

Taiglach are small, sticky-on-the-outside, crispy-in-the-centre, biscuits that are cooked in syrup and are notoriously difficult to make. They were my mother's specialty, and she prided herself on the fact that she could virtually turn them out in her sleep.

Among her circle of friends, she was known as The Taiglach Queen. Whenever there was a special occasion – a birth, a bar mitzvah, a wedding – or at *Pesach* or *Rosh Hashana* (Jewish New Year), my mother would be counted on to provide the taiglach.

I can still hear her muttering happily to herself in Yiddish while making a batch for a friend's daughter's wedding: *Gerotene taiglach, Gerotene kalah* (successful taiglach, successful bride) – as if the success of the marriage was somehow linked to the success of the batch of her taiglach.

Soon after my sister's marriage in Israel in 1970, my mother shipped from South Africa cartons of household items to her – pots and pans and linen, her modern-day trousseau, so to speak. Right at the top of the very last carton was a sealed container of freshly baked taiglach. The accompanying note – in Hebrew and English – for the customs officials read:

> These are for my daughter's wedding – feel free to take just one for yourself and please leave the rest for her.

Making taiglach was a mission. First, you had to make the dough, and roll out the individual biscuits. When I was young, my mother used to stuff these with dried fruit, and plait or roll them into balls. I remember 'helping' her – rolling and plaiting and re-rolling and re-plaiting my one small ball of dough while she prepared dozens. In later years, she simplified the process, dispensing with the filling and making simple bagel shapes.

The dough had then to be left outside on trays in the sun, to dry and crack. Then a huge pot (kept especially for this purpose) was filled with syrup, water, sugar, and ginger, and brought to a roaring boil on the stove. The biscuits were thrown into the boiling syrup, the lid clapped on and we watched with bated breath while steam poured out under the lid which could not be opened *under any circumstances* for the first twenty minutes.

Then came the moment of truth. As the lid was lifted, she would sigh with relief at the sight of puffy, risen and golden dough rings bubbling in the boiling syrup. She would quickly stir them, close the lid and keep repeating this process every few minutes, until they were pronounced done. Of course, this 'doneness' was where the magic occurred – knowing the exact moment when the biscuit was 'done enough' for the taiglach to be crisp and hold their shape without collapsing, but not 'too done', which would render them hard and impossible to eat.

Etched in my memory forever is the exact way she would test for this point by carefully cutting one syrupy biscuit in half and placing it on a saucer, balancing the sticky spoon on a separate saucer in a puddle of water. After a short wait to see that it didn't 'fall in', we would be allowed a tiny taste. If it was perfect, there would be a flurry of activity – boiling water added to the pot, ginger stirred in, and the biscuits rapidly spooned out of the pot onto waiting cooling racks, pools and puddles of syrup dripping everywhere! Finally, the taiglach would be rolled in desiccated coconut or sugar, cooled and stored.

And then the monumental clean-up of the sticky surfaces and syrup-encrusted pot would begin. But it was, without a doubt, worth every intricate minute.

Over the years, my sister and I both attempted making taiglach many times. We had, separately and together, often watched our mother making them, and we tried to write down her recipe step by step – itemizing the quirks and measuring meticulously the little bit of this and the little pinch of that, that led to perfection.

But no matter how often we tried, we never quite succeeded.

A few days after my mother's death, my sister and I were sorting through her papers and possessions. Amid the tears and laughter, and steeped in the essence of her, we found a piece of paper, in her easily recognizable handwriting: The Taiglach Recipe.

We pored over it in delight, vowing to make copies of the definitive recipe for the whole family. This recipe was a treasure – something to be kept for posterity. Only a few hours later, as we continued to sort through her papers, a second taiglach recipe appeared, and then a third, and after that, a fourth. Four versions of my mother's 'special' taiglach recipe, each slightly different from the others. It seems she too was trying to commit the perfect version of taiglach to paper!

Despite all my knowledge and the multitude of 'definitive recipes', I have never quite produced my mother's *perfect* taiglach. Somehow, that spark of Bobba magic continues to elude me.

***

After my father died, my mother retired from The Shop and lived alone in an apartment in Johannesburg. There she cooked to her heart's content.

My husband's sister, who lived in the adjacent apartment, recalls how Bobba would often be hovering near her door, when she came home, to welcome her with a slice of freshly baked apple pie and cream. The grandchildren all talk, to this day, of 'Bobba's amazing potato *latkes*', or her sensational *cheese blintzes* – mounds of crepes piling up between checked tea towels, while she slaved simultaneously over two frying pans, working so frantically in the heat she would inevitably get a nose bleed.

My mother was a chaotic cook with a trail of mess around her. She would produce vast quantities of everything in her tiny, overstuffed kitchen, moving from one task to the next in a blur of activity. She couldn't bear to throw anything out, so in addition to whatever she set out to make, there was always more – using up the leftovers from this to create that, and baking just one more thing, since it would be a pity to waste the hot oven.

Occasionally, she would jot down someone's recipe on the back of an envelope or a shopping docket, but if she ever found it, or tried to use it, she inevitably ignored half the ingredients, added others and made it her own.

Like when a friend of mine, who makes beautiful light scones, gave my mom her much-loved, tried and tested three-ingredient recipe. Sometime later, my mother served us *her* version. She had added 'just a little butter, sugar, egg, fruit and spices', and baked them in muffin pans. Suffice to say they bore no resemblance in taste, texture – or even ingredients – but were forever after, in her mind, 'Suzanne's scones'.

My mother didn't believe in expensive ingredients. To this day, I feel her eyes on me when I buy exorbitantly priced fresh salmon and tuna – I hear her mantra:

> Fish is fish – so why would you buy fancy fish when you could buy the cheapest, chop it, season it well and fry it – or boil as *gefilte* – and it would taste delicious.

She stockpiled when food was cheap, and made do when it wasn't. She didn't own a cookbook – cooking instead from her heart and her head, calling on her experience, instinct, memory and innovativeness.

Generally this led to wonderful food, but sometimes there were weird culinary disasters that she never acknowledged as such. Her tendency to never throw anything out, and to substitute ingredients with what was on hand, made for a few legendary tales.

My mother baked *challah* (a traditional plaited loaf for the Sabbath) every Friday, as her mother had done before her, and as I do now. Her *challahs* were beautiful – perfectly-plaited, sweet and golden and they melted in your mouth.

Every Shabbat meal began with Bobba's *challah*. Her grandchildren would wait impatiently for the blessing on the wine and bread to be completed so they could hoe into the warm bread. But on one memorable Shabbat, the *challah* was inedible – a nauseating grittiness replaced the usual sweet butteriness. And on inspection, the slices had a distinct green hue. Everyone sputtered and gagged, trying to find a polite way to spit out the awful bread without offending Bobba.

Bobba was not offended. In fact, she was totally unperturbed by the fuss. She continued eating, explaining she had run out of flour and had substituted perfectly good pea flour which she considered an improvement, since the increased vegetable content was sure to make it healthier!

***

At the age of seventy-seven, my mother went on a two-month study tour to Israel. She spent the night with her cousin, Zelda, in Tel Aviv, before her flight back to Australia.

Despite living in separate countries and very seldom seeing each other, the two women were extremely close. They were first cousins – Zelda's mother and Lea's father were siblings. When her mother died soon after giving birth, Zelda was raised by my grandmother, breastfed alongside my mother's brother, Hymie. In addition, these cousins shared something that connected them even more than genes and mother's milk. They were both survivors. Each had lost a husband and a young son in the concentration camps, and each had somehow, separately, made it out of the death camps and into new lives.

Two peas in a pod, they were infused with equal measures of love, loss, strength and determination. Not to mention a fiercely competitive spirit, and more than a little covert sibling rivalry.

Picture the scene, then, when my mother – the esteemed visitor – arrived for dinner, bringing with her a barbecued, kosher chicken she had bought along the way. Zelda was utterly insulted and bitterly offended that the delicacies she had spent all week preparing were not good enough. Incensed, she threatened not to let my mother in. No amount of explanation about the alluring smell and the novelty of readily available kosher food in Israel, made any difference.

Eventually, my mother managed to smooth the ruffled feathers, but nothing on earth could get that chicken onto Zelda's table. Her cousin flatly refused to have anything to do with it, and my mother – pathologically unable to discard anything edible – refused to throw it out. The only 'rational' way to end the stand-off was to freeze the chicken overnight, and for my mother to take it on the plane with her the next morning, when she flew back to Australia.

My mother's hand-luggage was heavy. She had with her the spoils of two months in Israel: books and memorabilia from the conference she had attended, and gifts for everyone back home. Stuffed into her large carry bag were also items too valuable for her checked luggage – silver candlesticks, Israeli jewellery, and *Tefillin* and *Tallit* for her two grandsons, who would both celebrate Bar-Mitzvahs that year. And, amongst all this, of course, a frozen, kosher chicken which she somehow managed to convince the air hostess to stow in the freezer of the tiny galley.

En route to Australia, she changed flights in Athens. Having dragged her heavy hand-luggage on to the plane, suffering from the heat and exertion, she began to feel unwell. Noticing her profuse sweating and pallor, the staff insisted she be examined by a doctor before allowing her to fly, and they escorted her, protesting loudly, off the plane. The *only* item of luggage she took with her in the drama and commotion, was the frozen chicken. By the time she had been examined and pronounced fit to fly, her scheduled flight had departed, and so she was taken to a local hotel where the airline put her up for the night. With the chicken safely in the hotel freezer.

When she boarded the flight for Australia the following day, the chicken was therefore the only thing that accompanied her. No clothes, no souvenirs, no memorabilia – just a kosher, frozen chicken.

Finally, after her 24-hours delay, emotional and exhausted, my mother made it back to Australia. On arrival, her still-frozen companion was immediately confiscated by the customs official and, in accordance with the country's strict quarantine laws, dumped into the nearest bin. Despite howls of protest, cajoling, pleading, accusing and every other negotiating trick she knew, my mother failed to retrieve the chicken.

Forever after, she would tell anyone who asked, that the customs official had 'stolen' her chicken, to eat it himself. And she never, ever, conceded that the symptoms she experienced in Athens were precursors to the mild heart attack she suffered the following week. For as long as she lived, she blamed it all on the stress caused by that hapless Israeli chicken.

CHAPTER 13.
FOOD IN THE GHETTO

(KOVNO, LITHUANIA, 1941–1943)

Almost twenty years after her death, I hear her – peering over my shoulder as I guiltily tip the scraps of dinner into the bin. 'A whole family, in the Ghetto, could survive a month on what you throw out!' she says accusingly.

NOT JUST A SURVIVOR

In 1941, Lithuania had been under Russian occupation for a year. The existence of a non-aggression pact between Germany and Russia (signed in 1939) had lulled the Jewish citizens of Lithuania into a false sense of security. Despite an awareness that German occupation in Poland and other areas were problematic, and that times were 'not good', life continued relatively normally.

In Kovno, most food was generally available, although much of it was in short supply, and there were long queues. The Hebrew school where my mother had been teaching had been closed, but she found work as a cashier at the Russian Government Bank where her husband was working as a foreign correspondent. Meanwhile, her mother-in-law looked after her young child. With both of them working, they lived reasonably well.

My mother's sister was also living in Kovno, so their parents visited from Malat whenever they could. During one of these visits, my mother spent hours in the food queues, trying to get something good for dinner. Her father had requested she buy meat. When she came home with only vegetables, he offered her money, thinking she might not have been able to afford meat, which was expensive. Quietly she explained to him that, despite many stores and many queues, the only meat available was pork.

My mother would rather have starved than bring pork into her home at any time – all the more so in the presence of her parents who were observant Jews. None of them had ever strayed from the Jewish dietary laws of *Kashrut*, where pork was strictly forbidden.

Her father sat silent for a long time, contemplating the choices. Then, resolute, he said 'Your child needs good food. Tomorrow, you will go again and stand in the queue. And you will try to buy meat, whatever kind that is available. Let the sin be on my head'.

It is stories like this that lead me to believe that the pragmatism and flexibility that fuelled my mother's instinct for survival, was ingrained in her genes.

***

On the weekend of the 20th June 1941, her father again came to visit her in Kovno. He had come to say goodbye, because the restaurant and land her parents owned in Malat led the ruling Russians to perceive of them as 'wealthy Jews' and they were facing deportation. But fate intervened, and deportation never happened. Instead, two days later, the Germans invaded and quickly occupied Kovno.

As soon as the Germans arrived, the Lithuanians, who had been secretly conspiring with them, attacked the Jews. This was their revenge against a people they believed was responsible for Russia occupying Lithuania. They rampaged against the Jewish citizens of Kovno, killing and torturing them in their homes and on the streets. Ten thousand Jews were killed by the Lithuanians during that first week of German occupation. Many Jewish families survived by going into hiding, including my mother and her family.

Eventually, the German authorities took over from the Lithuanians, and rounded up the local Jews, forcing them into the small area of the city they designated as the Ghetto.

The Kovno Ghetto was in a suburb named Slabodka. It was where the *Yeshivas* (Jewish religious seminaries) had been, and the people who lived there were mainly Jews. The preparation of the Ghetto by the Germans involved closing off streets and building electrified fences with guarded gates. Then Jews from other suburbs were forced to move into the Ghetto, leaving behind their possessions and their homes, which were looted and occupied by non-Jews evacuated from Slabodka and elsewhere in Kovno.

As part of their preparation, the German authorities commandeered buses to take outsiders back to their villages, and with the help of friends, my mother's sister and father secured passage back to Malat, where they, and all the Jews in their community, were murdered some months later.

My mother and her family, together with about thirty thousand other Jews, moved into the Ghetto, incarcerated in a suburb that had been designed for eight thousand. Those in the Ghetto who were among the original occupants of Slabodka were generally in a better position, as they had many of their possessions still in their homes.

But others, like my mother, were in a less fortunate predicament. During their week of hiding, my mother's apartment in down-town Kovno had been totally ransacked – every last one of their possessions had disappeared. So when she and Mokka arrived in the Ghetto, they came with nothing but the clothes on their backs – no possessions, no

FOOD IN THE GHETTO

money, no food. The family of four were accommodated in the entrance hall of a one-roomed apartment whose primary occupant was a young woman they had once befriended. In addition, the apartment housed the woman's married sister and husband, and another sister.

Despite the unbearably cramped living conditions, despite the torture and murders they had witnessed, despite the indescribable loss of everything they owned – especially their liberty – they felt lucky to have survived together.

Food in the Ghetto was scarce and within a very short time, the overriding concern became hunger. Mokka, with many other forced laborers, was working on rebuilding the nearby airfield. What he earned was barely enough to sustain them.

Because my mother had a small child, she was not allocated any work by the *Judenraht*, so she earned nothing and therefore had nothing with which to buy or barter for food. Her solution was to become 'an angel' – someone who worked illegally on behalf of someone else.

There was an older, wealthier woman who had lived in Slabodka before it became the Ghetto. She was allocated work by the *Judenraht* which she was obliged to do – it was an order, not a choice. She paid my mother to do it in her stead. In this role, my mother was sometimes required to do personal work for the Lithuanian or German guards at the airfield – to warm their food, or wash or darn their clothes. She was sometimes rewarded for this work with food, but generally received nothing.

Occasionally she worked with the men on the airfield, pouring cement. Although it was hard work, it enabled her to barter – in a very limited capacity – with some of the Lithuanians who worked there as well. She could trade items supplied by the woman for whom she was a stand-in, for food or money, and share the proceeds with her. In this way, she was able to put 'food' (potato peel soup and bread were staples) on the table.

Eventually the *Judenraht* agreed to give her some regular work in her own capacity, and she was sent to work – with sixty-five others – in a brick factory. The factory was a six kilometre walk from the Ghetto, in a rural area where there were a number of small villages and farms, so on the way to and from work, there were many opportunities to trade possessions from the Ghetto for food. The factory workers bribed the guards at a side gate into the Ghetto, and for the most part, this enabled them to bring things back into the Ghetto at the end of the day. In this way, the sixty-five people who worked at the brick factory managed to smuggle in food to feed many of the Ghetto inhabitants for eight months.

My mother and her family survived incarceration in the Ghetto, despite *selektions*, despite hunger and despite deprivation of freedom. They survived together until the day that they agreed to go to Estonia, as a family, only to discover that the offer of remaining together was simply another cruel Nazi hoax.

CHAPTER 14.
FOOD IN THE CAMPS

(ESTONIA AND GERMANY, 1943–1945)

We were put on a prefabricated train, one hundred women alone in a carriage. The men were sent somewhere else. My child was taken with my mother-in-law and I never saw them alive again. We travelled three days in locked carriages without food, water or toilet facilities, so you can imagine what I looked like when the carriages were opened. Those who survived were walked to the German acceptance station.

The very first thing – we had to undress. There were standing men, and German soldiers and some Jewish men, and they had to cut our hair, shave our hair and our bodies. You can just imagine what it means to young women, young girls, that all of a sudden, they have to undress in the face of men, strangers, and be shaven all over their bodies. If there was a hole that I could fall in, or somebody would shoot me, I would have been very happy at that stage. I just didn't know what to feel and how to react. I probably wasn't even mentally capable of understanding it.

I had very nice, brownish locks, beautiful hair. When it came to my turn, a German woman that was there came up and she said in German 'when I cut beautiful hair, I am doubly happy.' And she cut out here in the middle – right in the middle here – a big chunk. And afterwards, some men shaved me and we went into a bath house. It was already very cold, October, the beginning of winter. We had to leave all our clothing there and when we came out, we were given a striped dress – no underwear, nothing – and wooden clogs, these Holland wooden clogs, and you had to be very quick to get your size because everyone was grabbing. And then we had to put on that dress and put your feet into the wooden clogs.

We had to get to a table and they registered our name and they gave us a number. We came in as human beings, and came out as a number. No name, no nothing. I was number 1885 and that was that.

FOOD IN THE CAMPS

My mother's description of life in the concentration camps is harrowing. She started off in Vaivara on 26 October 1942 and was liberated from Bergen-Belsen on 15th April 1945. In the course of those two-and-a-half years she spent time in six camps in total – moving from Vaivara to Erida, then Lagedy, Stutthof and Ochsenzoll, before arriving in Bergen-Belsen in the month before liberation.

In one of her interviews, she described her first meal on arriving in Vaivara – after the trauma of separation from her child and husband, three days on a train with no food, water, or sanitation, and the degradation of being stripped, shaved and reduced to a number.

> In the evening, ten loaves of bread were brought in and buckets of brown water supposed to be tea or coffee. A woman was chosen to cut up the bread for one hundred people. Two hundred hungry eyes were watching. Some thought that some portions were bigger, others smaller. You cut off from one and put on the other. Eventually, when all agreed that the portions were almost equal, one woman turned with her back to the table and placed a finger on a portion and a second woman, also standing with the back to the table holding a list of the numbers, called a number and that portion was given to the woman whose number it was. You can imagine how long it took until we got our first piece of bread after four days of hunger.

Hunger was a constant companion. Some days, my mother said, she ate grass and stones to fill her empty stomach. Some days she survived on snow. Most days, the only food to be had was bread and watery soup.

Bread distribution was a very important event in our lives. Each person dealt differently with the piece of bread. Some ate it up immediately, drank some of the available liquid and went to sleep. Others ate half and saved the other half to take along to work the next day. But very often you woke in the night and ate it. I can tell you from experience that the awareness of that piece of bread tucked away under a corner of your straw, did not let you sleep in peace. Firstly, you were afraid that someone would pinch it, and secondly it just made you feel hungry. Others played with their piece of bread, licking it now and again until it melted away. Those were the worst off as they didn't feel that they had eaten at all, and the bread was gone.

Before the food was distributed, the SS guards encouraged their dogs to lick the fat, or extract whatever scraps they found in the soup troughs, before allowing the inmates to collect their rations. Every behaviour was designed to add degradation to starvation.

Maintaining hunger among the inmates served two purposes. Firstly – it was economical to have forced labour that required no expenditure on food. People were simply expendable – you worked, flogged and starved them

FOOD IN THE CAMPS

to death, literally, and when they were spent, they were replaced. And secondly, it reinforced their worthlessness.

Now the pattern of their program was the same in all the countries that they have conquered. In all the concentration camps where the Jews were brought in, the destruction of the human angle was their first aim. They had really aimed at firstly dehumanising us, to make us animals. Their sadism was satisfied when they saw that two Jews were fighting over a piece of bread, or over the stump of a cigarette, or something like that.

They just wanted us, first of all, to feel that we are no more human. When they took away our names, and they gave us numbers, they were saying: *you are worthless*. And they were always telling us that we are vermin, we are worth being treated like vermin, we are nothing. And you know, if you think about our normal everyday life, it's very, very difficult to hurt or to kill a person. It's probable a little bit easier, but still not easy, to kill or hurt one of our pets. But it is nothing to kill a fly or some other little crawling creature.

This was actually psychologically how the young Germans were brought up. The Nazis were converting us into flies so that the German soldiers, even their citizens, lost their sensitivities to us as people, and found it easy to kill us. When they are not dealing

> anymore with masses of human beings, but just vermin – they can kill, they can torture, they can do whatever they like. There are no feelings attached to it.

But my mother was physically and mentally strong, smart and resourceful, and she had a powerful driving force – to survive.

> The only way that you could carry on living, was when you just didn't think. You became dehumanised. You just imagined that you are no more human, but you are just alive. Whatever the case is, no matter how terrible the circumstances – the filth, the hunger, the cruelty, the suffering – you just live. And if you want to survive, so you just have to look after one thing, after one centre in your life to which no one from outside can get. By that I mean a self within you – *your self* – your morals, your memories that you brought from home, whatever you once were, you have got to keep it within yourself, and try not to forget it, and try not to let it get lost.

The part of her that remained within her 'dehumanised self' was, to a large extent, linked with food – and tied up with that, the desire to help others, to support them and to uplift them, and to pull them along with her in her quest for survival.

FOOD IN THE CAMPS

When we were very, very hungry, we spoke about food. We were talking about Pesach and *kneidlach* and *kishke* and *tzimmes* and what not, just to forget our circumstances. And we were really satisfied with that which we spoke about – we just felt the taste of it. We forgot – we tried to forget – where we are when we could. And those that could not do it, when they reached a stage where they couldn't even daydream of better times, or past times, or they have forgotten of it already, they did not survive.

I remember one year, in 1944, we had a *seder* (a traditional Jewish Passover meal). There were frozen potatoes. You know in Germany they used to bury the potatoes into a big ditch for the winter, so when they opened those ditches, the top row was covered with straw and the potatoes at the top were frozen. Now they couldn't eat those frozen potatoes, because they are sweet and if you keep them for a little bit longer, they've got a bad taste. So they gave us those potatoes. We took them to our camp, the potatoes, and we cut round little slices. We had in our barracks one little coal stove, so we cut little round slices of potato, and we baked it on the coal stove, and those were our *matzos*. We really had a *seder*. We baked those potatoes, and we pretended that we've got cold drinks, and we made *seder*. And whoever remembered something about *mitziat mitzrayim* (the leaving of Egypt), recited it. And we were talking about our own *mitziat mitzrayim* – that one day we would be freed.

***

Over the course of the 30 months in the concentration camps, there was always hunger – sometimes more, sometimes less. When she worked in the kitchen in Vaivara, my mother had access to a little extra food that she would share, or with which she could bargain. And when she was sent to the Ochsenzoll work camp near Hamburg, there was generally more food available, and better conditions, and here she built enough reserves with which to withstand the almost total starvation she experienced in Bergen-Belsen.

Ochsenzoll was the second last camp my mother was sent to. She was there for eight months. An offshoot of the infamous women's only Ravensbrück concentration camp, it was a small, new camp that housed three hundred women who were part of an involuntary labour force for a nearby ammunition factory. It was a privately-owned factory – *Hansiatishes Ketten Werk* – that normally produced chains, but had been requisitioned by the German war government and re-purposed to make ammunition. It was still run by civilians – the factory supervisor, (the *Obermeister*) and a young engineer, who oversaw the production line where my mother worked. The Obermeister was a kindly, old man, and the young engineer was quite relaxed – happy to be in civilian work and not sent to the front.

The factory comprised a number of halls, each producing some different form of ammunition. Each hall employed women from one of the barracks. My mother worked in Hall Five, where they produced bullets. The private owners of the factory were paid three marks per labourer per day, and thus, in order to keep them productive – and of maximum economic value – the factory owners ensured that the women experienced comparatively good conditions.

Each of the barracks housed 24 women per room. In each room, there were eight cots of three levels, and each woman had her own bunk – a relative luxury. A loaf of bread was shared between six, rather than the customary ten, and the women's heads remained unshaven.

The *Lager Fuhrer* at Ochsenzoll was a retired air force captain who was recalled from retirement by the Nazi government, when there were no younger men available, and put in charge of the camp. He was a good man, and treated the inmates well.

The *Lager Fuhrer* was very, very good to me – very good to our whole camp. He saw that we haven't got real shoes, and we haven't got this or that, and he was bringing for us from the closed Hamburg theatres, all the clothes that were there. He told us to find dressmakers, amongst our group there, and to fit up the dresses for ourselves. And he saw to it that we should get some shoes. He was always looking for some more food for us – going in the villages there and bringing some cabbages and some frozen potatoes and some other things for us. But he was doing it very carefully – he was afraid. In the end, this didn't help him much. The *Blitzwomen* eventually sent a letter that he's too good to us, and eventually, he was sent away. He was sent away himself to some camp.

While this *Lager Fuhrer* was in charge of the camp, things were relatively good. Initially, my mother was one of twenty women selected to work in the camp itself, rather than in the factory. After a few days, while working in the kitchen, the *Lager Fuhrer* came in, and they conversed in German. He decided to put her in charge of one of the work groups that operated in Hall Five. Each day she had to select sixty women and take them to the factory, and supervise their activity on the production line. As part of her work, my mother used to go to a little office overlooking the hall, where she would register her workers. During the day shift, there was an old German woman who worked in that office and my mother was always polite to her, and sometimes went to talk to her. Over time she came to like my mother, and would secretly leave a sandwich or an apple in the desk drawer for her – always careful not to be seen to be helping her.

Making bullets was a complicated process. There were thirteen zones of the production line, starting with a wooden template and a sheet of steel, and ending with a completed box of bullets, that got sent away. My mother said she was quite sure that the bullets they produced never killed anybody, because they were always faulty, and were returned to the factory to be re-worked and remade again and again.

> It wasn't sabotage, but just we didn't know what to do – I mean women, ladies and girls, they never worked on this – they never knew what to do. This had to be done with very strict proportion and all – and it wasn't. At some point, they needed some parts, and there was such a disorder, you couldn't get the part, so one of the mechanics took me to that place and was teaching me to make the parts. He says you have got enough time, after you register you come and you make a few parts. What I knew about the parts – ha! But he was teaching me and I was making.

Each morning, the women from all the barracks who worked in the factory collected on the assembly field, before moving off to the production halls. My mother had all the information about her hall (how many women each production zone required, and the numbers – not names – of the allocated women and so on) written in a book. Her shift changes were always smooth and quick and there were no hitches. One morning, while standing at the assembly, ready to call her women, it began to rain heavily so she couldn't take out her book. She nevertheless called out every individual's given number and production zone requirement, relying only on memory. The *Lager Fuhrer*, who was watching, was impressed, and soon after he approached her with a plan.

> There was such a disorder there with the machine parts, nobody could ever find what was needed. They were always remaking things that they had but couldn't find. So he said to me: 'You know, Lily' – he used to call me Lily, 'I want to put you in the office, and you make a catalogue, and sort out all the parts here that are in such a mess, put them in order and sort them all out, and then we'll know what to find where. But you can't work in the office dressed like this'. So he chose for me a maroon velvet dress somewhere, and a dressmaker had to fit it for me, and I was very nicely dressed up in a maroon velvet dress. My hair had started to grow out, so I had a short haircut. So he met me there – in the office – one day in the morning, and at that stage there were long tables and there were six German women working there during the day.
>
> He said: 'This is Lily, and she's going to work here, and make a catalogue for the factory'. But one German young woman, a civilian, I don't remember her name (but I remember her face), she objected. She refused to have me sit with them at the table, and she made a whole fuss about it, and I had to be taken away and I couldn't work there. The factory catalogue never happened.

At the time, the *Lager Fuhrer* had devised a quota system for productivity, as a thinly-veiled cover to provide his workers with food in addition to their rations. He couldn't simply hand out the extra food he was sourcing for them as he was already under suspicion (in the end, he was reported for berating a *Blitzwoman* for stealing jam from the inmates), so he had to find a different way: when a production team achieved the quota target, they were rewarded with extra food.

Unable to catalogue the factory, my mother was put to work assisting the '*Tzeller-meister*' – a man in charge of keeping records of the numbers and specifications of the bullets produced each day. Because he was old, and partially blind, he handed over the task of recording to her, which gave my mother the opportunity she needed. Once she started recording ammunition production, all the teams suddenly began achieving their quotas – because in her records, the same boxes of bullets simply recirculated again and again, each time being registered as a new batch.

> And nobody worried about it. The young engineer who was working with our Hall, also didn't worry about it – whether we are working, or we are not working, we are producing or not producing, as long as he can stay here and not go to the front, he was happy.

***

In this way – with the help of a little extra food – the women of Ochsenzoll were all able to recuperate a little. They ate better, they slept better, and their morale improved. They were treated as humans, and in a way, felt valued. But eventually, their luck ran out. Their *Lager Fuhrer* was reported and sent away. And his replacement was a terror.

A new young German *Lager Fuhrer* came. He could take a woman, I don't know, what she did, how she mispleased him, and he would put her head down into a kettle of water – or send a woman into the electric wires – that's what he was doing. To him it meant nothing, to kill a person, it meant nothing.

Once, when I argued with him about something, he said to me, 'You are like a fly. To squash a fly into the wall is the same thing as to kill one of you'. That's what he often said.

Once I was caught smoking in the kitchen. The people that were delivering some things were smoking cigarettes, and throwing away a piece of it, a piece of cigarette. So the girls in the kitchen there, they were collecting the pieces of cigarettes, and we were wrapping it in some newspaper, and every day we shared a smoke. One of the *Blitzwomen* walked in and

FOOD IN THE CAMPS

she saw that I was smoking. I threw it away but she saw it. Even though I begged her, and she promised not to tell, the moment the *Lager Fuhrer* walked in, she told him.

The next morning he called me, and demanded the name of the person who had given me the cigarette. I told him that we just found the bits and wrapped it up, but he kept torturing me with a sharp triangular piece of steel, poking and poking and poking the skin here, next to my eye, continuously, interrogating me to give him a name. In the end, because I wouldn't give him a name, he became very angry, but I was lucky that he didn't kill me. He eventually gave up and he sent me away. I still have the scar.

On Sunday mornings, when the factory was closed, the *Lager Fuhrer* would force them to clean the streets, in Hamburg, wiping the soot from the nightly bombardment off the buildings. My mother recalled how they would sit in the barracks watching with glee as the bombs were falling on Hamburg and the city was burning.

But as the war progressed, there was no more steel available to make bullets and the factory was permanently closed. So the three hundred women were sent to Bergen-Belsen.

***

Bergen-Belsen was a large concentration camp close to the border between Germany and Poland. In March 1945 as the end of the war neared, and Nazi defeat became an inevitability, the Nazi's began gathering people from all the surrounding camps and sending them to Bergen-Belsen to die. It was a place where the Nazis didn't need to do much to kill – the camp was infested with typhus, and with no food, no space, and no sanitation, inmates there simply died in their hundreds every day.

The afternoon when the camp leader came to tell us that tomorrow morning at 4 o'clock you must be ready to go; he didn't tell us that we are going to Bergen-Belsen. 'I am going to send you to a new camp,' he told the familiar story. 'You are not to take along the dishes' (you know we had a little bowl and a spoon, we had already arranged to have toothbrushes, this that and the other, you know women have little things). 'You mustn't take anything along because you are going to a very nice new camp, and you will find there everything for you prepared'. And he kept on and on that we must not take along anything. So we were sure that we are going to be sent to Auschwitz.

And none of us slept that night, and at 4 o'clock we were all up and they took us to the railways. The management of our factory did not let us walk the death walk like from all the other places, they sent us by train.

I don't know for what reason they did it. I think that our supervisor, the civilian *Obermeister* of that factory, a very nice, decent old man, I think it was probably his doing that he decided that they have got to treat their workers well, and they sent us by train.

Now, it is a distance of three hours by train, but the train couldn't get through. You come to some place and there you can't pass, you've got to go back, you've got to go on other rails, because the war was on and the Russians were near and the Allies were bombarding all the time. The train shunting forwards and backwards, and forwards and backwards and we were travelling like that for four days, without food, until we arrived.

During that train trip we saw the people marching in the thousands, the thousands of our dying brethren – we saw them – and I still see it – I still can't get over it. They were lying in the snow, it was March. It was snowing all over. People just black, you couldn't see the skin on them, lying with their hands out, water, water, water – a bit of water, a bit of water a bit of snow, a bit of something. They couldn't move, and they were just left and the Germans were passing by. The German guards with their rifles, if they saw that the ones were really screaming or crying, they would just shoot them, and the others they just ignored them, just left them. It did not matter to them whether they were humans lying there – it was nothing. Nothing mattered.

When the train finally arrived – everyone started to run back. Nobody wanted to be the first to leave. So we said goodbye to each other. I said goodbye to my little girl, and my cousin, and said goodbye to the world. And when we were sure we were going to go to the gas chamber, when the carriage opened, we nearly fell out. I don't know how I stood on my feet – we were half-dead already. But we saw some camp inmates approaching, someone in striped clothes. And we went through the gate. The Nazi *Blitzwomen* did not come with us. They just remained behind, and we went in. They took us into the camp.

The barracks were all full – packed. There was no place where to sleep, nothing to eat – but somehow, we got a little place, where the three of us – this girl and my cousin and I – the three of us slept in one little corner. There was no food and no work and simply nothing. But this little girl of mine she went away and she came back with something. She took out from under her dress a little pumpkin which she had picked up around the kitchen under threat of death. The Germans were shooting, but she got there, and she got a little pumpkin. And we lived on this for four days.

FOOD IN THE CAMPS

Bergen-Belsen, that was the end. That was really the end of the world. There are no words to describe what Bergen-Belsen was like. It was winter, it was snow. Now in the barracks there were hundreds of people – lying on the bunks, under the bunks, in the passage, in the entrance – there was no door in the entrance – you couldn't get out, you couldn't get in. You could do nothing.

There were always bodies – you were climbing over bodies. As soon as somebody died, the people that were near them just pushed them out, threw them out the windows, and threw them into a heap. There were heaps lying all over, and in the night the snow covered it, creating pretty white mountains. Until April, when the snow started to melt. Now you can just imagine, think of it, tens of thousands of bodies were lying there all the time and when the snow melted, they were uncovered, starting to rot. That was Bergen-Belsen.

***

My mother, her cousin, and her 'adopted daughter' survived in Bergen-Belsen for five weeks. Then, on 12th April 1945, the entire camp leadership – the German guards, the *Kappos*, the *Blitzwomen* – everyone, left the camp. The inmates were locked inside. The grounds of the camp were mined and Hungarian SS guards were stationed around the electrified perimeter fences. These guards were instructed to blow up the camp and kill all of the inmates the following day at midday, if the German leaders had not returned by then. The Hungarian guards told some of the Hungarian inmates, and word spread, so by the following morning, everyone in the camp knew that the camp was going to be destroyed and that they were going to be killed that day.

But just before midday, the German leadership came back. They had been trying to flee the advancing armies of the Russians and the Allies – leaving the camp dressed in their civilian clothes and trying to cut through the woods surrounding Bergen-Belsen. But they were surrounded by the Russians and the Allies, and they couldn't get through. So they returned – all wearing white armbands with painted yellow skulls. They hoisted white flags with yellow skulls, advertising that the camp was infested with typhus, pretending to be nursing the sick and hoping the Allies would choose not to enter into a typhus-ridden camp. However, two days later, on 15th April 1945, the liberating Allies drove into the camp.

> We knew that something is going to happen and we are going to be either liberated or killed – something is going to happen to us. And on the 15th in the morning, they had switched off the electrifying fence – and we saw two motorbikes coming not through the gate, but straight through the fence, the motorbike jumped through the fence onto the *appelplatz*. We couldn't get

out through the door because the place was all blocked up with dead people – so a few of us, I – jumped out through the windows, to see what's happening. We knew that something was happening, and the uniforms of the two men that came onto the *appelplatz* weren't the German grey uniforms, they were beige. As we came out the windows onto the *appelplatz*, the German guards came forward to hit us, to chase us back. One of the two motorbike men came up to the guard and ripped off his epaulets and he said to us in English, 'Don't be afraid. You are free'.

And then, everybody else also came out through the windows, they started to, to kiss them, and then jeeps – jeeps with some military people came up, and there was a big noise. Meanwhile they have surrounded all the Germans that were there, they picked them all up, and the next morning we already saw that the Germans are busy carrying the dead people. The snow had melted, and there was a terrible stench from the uncovered half rotten bodies. Now these Germans were made to carry every single one of those bodies.

We saw them from far. They wouldn't let us come near to them, because we were shouting, and we wanted to throw stones, and we wanted to hit them, so they didn't let us near them. But we saw that they were working, carrying the dead. There was a little puddle, a little lake, a tiny little lake, and we were all standing around the lake and we saw that one of the guards jumped into the lake. But they pulled him out, they wouldn't allow him to escape by drowning.

And that, that was our liberation.

CHAPTER 15.
FOOD AFTER LIBERATION

(BERGEN-BELSEN, 1945)

After liberation, food took on a new meaning. Many people, on being liberated, died when they began eating – the ultimate tragedy. Having suffered starvation for so long they could not tolerate the reintroduction of a normal diet.

Indeed, my mother spent years learning to eat normally again. At the time of her liberation from Bergen-Belsen, my mother – a medium height, medium build woman – weighed under 70 pounds. She had spent the years from 1941 to 1945 in various degrees of starvation.

Immediately after liberation, Bergen-Belsen became a displaced persons camp caring for thousands of survivors. Although food was available, it was still in short supply and rationed. Among her papers, there is a certificate of the supplies my mother received. I remember her telling me how they used aspirin – medical supplies were plentiful – as a substitute for baking powder, when they were trying to bake a birthday cake.

Her initial three weeks after liberation were spent in and out of consciousness in hospital. But when she recovered, she started to work – first as secretary to the Commanding Officer of Bergen-Belsen camp, then for a short while for the Jewish council, and finally she was approached to start a kosher kitchen for the Jewish former inmates who remained in the camp.

> They want a kosher kitchen. The Hungarian Jews all wanted a kosher kitchen, and there was no one who could take it on, so I took it on. I got eight of my girls, of my group, (my adopted daughters that eventually went to live in Israel) and we made a kosher kitchen. And we were cooking there for three hundred people – you know, the people were all still there.

Although it was kosher, she was adamant that religious laws were not going to stand in the way of providing food. She wouldn't back down, even when the Rabbi insisted it was too close to sunset on the eve of the Sabbath to light the cooking fires, and consequently no hot food could be prepared.

> I said: 'Oh no, we hungered enough – we were hungry for years. I'm going to cook', I said, 'whether its Shabbat or it's not Shabbat, I have got to cook. And you go and find somewhere a loophole in the Torah that I can cook, because I am going to cook even if you don't allow

me and even if you don't agree, because I can't let the people be two days without food again.'

Finally, she was back doing what she did so well – cooking, feeding, and defending people, in her unwavering style.

PART FOUR:
EDUCATION

*My mother at her graduation –
University of Witwatersrand, Johannesburg, 1966*

My mother spent her entire life studying – it was her joy, her therapy, her identity, her rational way of dealing with an often-irrational world. She revered education. While other people admired beauty and wealth, she cherished intelligence and learnedness.

CHAPTER 16.
EDUCATION IN LITHUANIA

(1918–1935)

From an early age my mother exhibited amazing talent – for recall, for language, for numbers and for analytical thinking. While she was still a young child in Byutichik, her brother, Hymie and their cousin Zelda, (who was Hymie's age), were home-schooled by a Russian teacher at the estate. Six years their junior, she was too young for formal education, but she nevertheless always attended the lessons, and passively absorbed whatever they were being taught.

She first attended a real school in Malat.

> I started at a Hebrew school. I still remember when I came to school the teacher gave me some problem, some arithmetic problem, in Hebrew. I didn't know Hebrew – I knew Russian – my first languages that I spoke were Yiddish and Russian. So I said to him, 'translate it to me into Russian, then I'll know what it is'. So he did translate it, and I got the problems correct, and they put me into grade two. They put me into grade

two because I knew arithmetic, and I knew Russian, and I knew the alphabet, the Lithuanian alphabet, and a little bit of Lithuanian.

I struggled that year; I didn't know Hebrew. I still remember that my mother used to ask my school friends to come and to prepare the lessons together, with me, and she used to give them apples and fruit and buns and whatever they wanted, just to come and work with me.

So at the end of that year, I failed Hebrew. I passed all the other subjects, and I failed Hebrew. So I asked my father to get me a private Hebrew teacher for the holidays, which he did. And I still remember that I used to sit in a back room in our home, so as not to see that my friends are all going to swim in the heat of the summer. But I worked, and I passed the exam, and got into standard three or grade three or whatever they called it, and from then I got up and up and I was the best pupil when I finished the Primary.

There was no Hebrew high school in Malat, so when she completed primary school, my mother had to continue her studies in another town – Wilkomir (known in Lithuanian as Ukmerge). Her parents arranged for her to stay with a cousin, but she was terribly home sick and after a few months, they sent her home.

EDUCATION IN LITHUANIA

> That winter I stayed at home, but in the spring, my friends that went together with me to that school in Wilkomir, when they came home, all with their uniforms and their hats and all that, and I have to go back to standard four, they are already in five, it didn't suit me. So I asked again my father to get me a teacher, I want to work and to write the exams, and to get into standard five. He got a senior girl to teach me, and I worked very hard that whole summer and went back to that town, there, to High School, wrote all the exams that they wanted and passed into five. So I was with my friends and I was a very good pupil all the years of my High School. I passed with all distinctions that were available.

Right from the beginning she set the educational foundation for her life – to study hard in order to overcome any obstacles, and to excel as a consequence.

***

In 1932 my mother went to university in Kovno. She wanted to study medicine, and had the academic qualifications to do so, but there was a discriminatory quota system in place – a Jewish woman was the lowest priority – so she didn't get accepted. Instead, she studied Biology, which in those days was an achievement in itself, as very few women attended university, or even completed high school.

As part of this degree, she studied many medical subjects, hoping this would enable her to transition to medicine. But no place in the medical school became available, and after 3 years she graduated with a degree in Natural Sciences and proceeded to teach Botany and Zoology at a high school for a year.

Although Natural Science was not her primary choice, my mother loved what she studied – particularly Botany. Her entire life she loved gardening, plants and flowers. The garden at our home in Benoni, was her pride and joy, with beautiful roses, dahlias and hydrangeas flowering profusely every year. We always had fruit trees laden with apricots, lemons and figs, which she pruned and nurtured in her own classic way, and with her own fixed ideas. The citrus trees all had metal nails tapped into their trunks 'to give them iron' and garlic was planted around the base 'to prevent cut-worms'.

She also believed that 'good gardening' involved removing any low undergrowth, to give plants maximal opportunity to grow without anything competing for the nutrients in the soil. This idea prompted her to prune my garden in Durban – unasked – during one of her regular visits. I returned home from work, to discover my beautiful, lush fan palm had been converted into a telephone pole with three miserable fronds right at the top.

> I removed all the unnecessary leaves around the whole trunk. It will grow beautifully, now.

***

Her love of nature logically endorsed the healing power of plants, and long before it became fashionable to do so, my mother was always ready to try the latest plant-based remedy – with her own little twist. She adhered to the principle that 'if a little is good, more is better'. When she read that celery seed tablets were good for arthritis, she incorporated generous quantities of celery into every dish she prepared. It wasn't in her nature to look for the convenience of a celery seed capsule. Instead, she simply consumed bunches and bunches of raw celery every day.

The same applied to garlic, which she had always loved. She explained that even while starving in the camps, she would gladly give up a day's ration of bread for a tiny nib of garlic, just so that it felt as if she were eating real food. And after food became plentiful once more, garlic was an inevitable ingredient in all her cooking. But when in later life she read of its alleged health properties, she went overboard, eating raw garlic to the extent that a Sydney bus driver once asked her – the only passenger – to move to the back of the otherwise empty bus, because he couldn't tolerate the potent garlic odour she exuded.

Her third 'plant medicine' obsession was ginger. Every morning she would drink hot water with freshly grated ginger. Even as an old lady she would stubbornly grate her own ginger with her arthritic hands, using an old hand grater. Grated ginger was readily available, but it was expensive, and however generous my mother was to us, she wouldn't spend unnecessarily on herself if there was a cheaper option.

Buderim Ginger is Australia's premium ginger plantation, and Buderim's ginger products are of the highest quality. After a visit to the ginger plantation, she finally agreed to allow me to buy a large bottle of grated ginger for her. She took one taste, and wrinkled her nose.

> Whatever it is in this bottle, it's not ginger. In fact, it hasn't even lain next to ginger!

And that was the end of that.

CHAPTER 17.
STUDY AS A PRACTICAL SOLUTION

(SOUTH AFRICA, 1947–1966)

My mother was a pragmatist. When there was a problem, she would solve it – first with her own brand of common sense, and if that was inadequate, she would simply go out and obtain a suitable academic qualification to facilitate the solution. Issues that presented at the different stages of her life were dealt with by obtaining diplomas: in Hebrew teaching, nursery school teaching, bookkeeping and remedial educational therapy, as well as various other less structured learning experiences.

Soon after she arrived in South Africa, once she was well enough, my mother realised she needed to work. She had reasonable conversational English, and she spoke Hebrew fluently. She had taught at a high school in the past, and teaching was therefore a logical choice in seeking employment. But she didn't want a full-time teaching job – she had decided to go back to study at University in the mornings, so she only wanted to work part-time. Teaching at a *Cheder* (afternoon Hebrew School) was the perfect option. So in addition to her University studies, she completed a Hebrew Teacher's Diploma in the evening, that then enabled her to teach *Cheder* two afternoons a week.

Just before my sister was born, she realised she would need greater flexibility than the *Cheder* job offered. She was about to graduate from University, freeing up her mornings – so she studied for a diploma to qualify as a Hebrew nursery school teacher. She subsequently ran the nursery school for those years in which she needed to bring her baby to work with her.

Soon after I was born, by which time my sister was ready to go to school, my mother changed direction again. She decided to become more involved in my father's business, to compensate for his lack of business acumen. Her intuition about expanding the range and appeal of the business proved correct, but her practical accounting skills were inadequate. She dealt with this by enrolling in a technical college, and did two night courses in bookkeeping.

And it didn't end there. As part of her Bachelor of Education Degree, she had studied remedial education, an area she really loved. Thus, in addition to running my father's business, and studying at University, and running a home, and looking after two young children, my mother decided to use her skill in remedial education to give private tutoring at our home in the evenings and Sunday mornings. This lasted for a few years, and then she stopped, deciding that she was unfairly compounding the learning problem of her students by teaching with her Yiddish accent.

CHAPTER 18.
STUDY AS THERAPY

(SOUTH AFRICA, 1947–1987)

Aside from the various diplomas she gathered as practical 'necessities', study – for my mother – was therapeutic. It gave her a reason to get up every day. It gave her an automatic reprieve from her daily grind. It filled her mind with thoughts other than of her experiences, and her loss. Study was a legitimate reason to withdraw from the world and immerse herself in something different. It was OK to say – 'I can't come, I'm studying' whereas it was considered unacceptable to say, 'I don't feel like being sociable.'

> In 1947 I just didn't know what to do. I was sick, and I was in hospital for a few months and when I came out of hospital, I just didn't know what to do with myself, all alone and always with nightmares, and I couldn't sleep at night. So my cousin said to me: 'What do you want to do? What should we try? To go back teaching?' I was a teacher, but I couldn't even think about teaching all day.

NOT JUST A SURVIVOR

And then I said – I'll teach twice a week, two hours in the afternoon. So what am I going to do in the morning, and the whole day, thinking all the time about the camps? I decided I want to go back to university. So I went back to university. I told them what I had studied and what I was, and I was accepted to do a B.A. I started in 1947, and I qualified in 1950.

When I was studying – when I was doing my B.A – I never slept in a bed. I was sitting at a table and doing my work. You see – in the morning I was at lectures, in the afternoon I went teaching, I was teaching two days, and afterwards I was teaching three afternoons – so at night I had to prepare essays and my university stuff. So I used to sit at the table and work, and fall asleep, and have a nightmare, and wake up, and carry on with my work, and fall asleep again and wake up again, and the next morning I am up and going to university. There I felt at home. There I was always so busy. And listening so hard. I was devoted to my studies. I was devoted with all my heart and all my soul. Because I had nothing – nothing else to think about – I didn't want to think about anything else. I just wanted to think about my studies.

In order to be accepted at university, my mother had to prove her prior education. But she had no documentation. She found two friends originally from Kovno, who were living in Johannesburg, who provided her with affidavits that she had been with them at high school and that she had attended university in Kovno, where she had completed her degree. Another friend, who had been her teacher at high school, attested to her successful high school career and entry to university. Her documents detailing that she was a survivor, and documenting her liberation from Bergen-Belsen were also taken into account, and the University of Witwatersrand approved her application.

At the time, she spoke only moderate English. She not only studied everything in English, but also undertook English as a major, together with German and Hebrew. She also studied Psychology, History of Art and History of Music. She struggled with the English, but she passed everything except her very first English exam. Devastated, she approached her lecturer, who explained to her that in the exam there had been optional question choices – my mother had attempted to answer every question and she inevitably ran out of time!

Over the course of her B.A. degree she made friends, and endeared herself to the members of the Faculty, who gave her wonderful references. They all commented on her diligence and dedication, and they recognised that her marks were lower than they should have been, mostly due to the limitations of her English. These references were used to get bursaries and funding for her further studies, but they were also essential for her self-esteem.

Because of my mother's Holocaust stories, I have always had difficulty hearing people – especially older people – speaking German. I automatically feel uncomfortable and wary and it is one of the reasons I will never visit

Germany. I expected that my mother would feel the same, and therefore found it odd that she had chosen to study German at University. When I asked her about this, she was surprised.

> I love the German language, its music and its poetry. It is familiar, and I spoke it well – so it was an advantage to study this at university. My issue was with Hitler and the Nazis – not the language or its culture.

Despite this, she never bought anything made in Germany and never voluntarily visited there. But she was, in some respects, surprisingly forgiving. She acknowledged that not all German people were to blame for the past, and she sometimes tried to find justification for the civilians who were by-standers to the atrocities she suffered. She was also always quick to acknowledge the few German people who were kind to her during her incarceration.

As part of her personal 'mission' to educate everyone about the Holocaust, my mother used to go to various High Schools, and give lectures to the students, and their history teachers. I remember her saying she had been to lecture to the students of a private German college in South Africa, and how hard it had been to ensure that she did not destroy the students' respect or love for their older German family members.

Despite her tolerance, and even though she tried to justify some of their behaviour, she never forgave the

STUDY AS THERAPY

German civilians for their role in facilitating the Holocaust. In later adult life, she received a reparation pension from the German Government. In order to receive this, she had to present herself to the appropriate authorities in Germany, to prove her identity, and justify her entitlement. She flew to Berlin, where a lawyer picked her up from the airport, drove her to the office, and completed the interview. She wryly commented that, with typical German fastidiousness, everything was organised and perfectly expedited, and that everyone she dealt with was polite and efficient. When the documents were signed, the lawyer offered to take her sight-seeing or shopping – anywhere she wanted for the next six hours, before her return flight. At that stage, she pointed to her feet that were dangling above the ground while she was seated, carefully avoiding the floor.

> I don't want my feet on German ground one second more than is absolutely necessary.

She spent the next six hours at the airport, on what she felt was relatively neutral international territory, feet off the ground, waiting to go home. That was the last time she was ever in Germany.

But she was happy to study, and speak, and listen to the German language, music, art and literature.

***

> So I finished my B.A. Then I'm again wondering what to do. I got married in 1948, and I had one baby, and afterwards another baby after a few years, and after the second baby, I have to do something, I have to go back to university. I just wasn't ready to do anything. So I went back to university, and in 1962, I started B.A. Honours. In 1965 I finished B.A. Honours.
>
> Then I am again free, for a couple of months, looking for this and looking for that. One day I was at the university and I saw there the office of the Education Department. So I walked into the Education Department, to see what's going on there. I spoke to the secretary and she said, 'you can do a master's degree here', but I decided I'd do a Bachelor of Education.

For her Bachelor of Education degree, my mother wrote a thesis entitled 'The History and Development of Jewish Education in the Transvaal'. The research for her Education thesis cemented her relationship with the Jewish Board of Deputies, the Jewish Board of Education and many other Jewish communal organisations. These relationships continued for the rest of her time in South Africa.

Before the advent of computers and word processors, a thesis was hand-written, and then professionally typed on a typewriter, with multiple copies being produced using carbon paper. A few copies were then bound and presented to the university. It was a laborious and time-consuming process.

My mother had completed the final, hand-written draft of her thesis and was taking it to the typist in Johannesburg. She was – as usual – in a hurry on that day. She had a number of things on her mind – things to return to the wholesalers while she was in the city, accounts for the accountant and so on, and she was – as usual – running late. So she jumped into her trusty little car and rushed off, forgetting that the hand-written thesis was stacked in an open carton and perched on the roof of her car. Halfway to Johannesburg it dawned on her that all the papers flying around her on the highway were her thesis.

Luckily, the penultimate hand-written draft had not yet been destroyed, and she laboriously wrote a new final copy. She graduated in 1967.

***

From the time of her arrival in South Africa, my mother was an integral member of almost every Jewish communal organisation she came into contact with. Any Zionist organisation or anything at all to do with the Holocaust, or Lithuanian Jewry in South Africa concerned her, and she invariably became involved – as a member, or a Board member, or the Chairlady. It was therefore a reasonable decision, when she once again enrolled at university – this time to do a P.H.D – to write a thesis that involved examining Jewish life and culture.

She decided to focus her research on Jewish life in Oriental Jewish communities, and her friend and mentor, Professor Rappaport, who was the head of the University of the Witwatersrand department of Jewish Studies at the time, was appointed her supervisor. As part of the P.H.D. requirement, she needed to be registered for three years before the thesis could be submitted.

But during those three years, things changed. In 1970 (partly influenced by discussions with her recently-acquired Moroccan-Israeli son-in-law), she changed the thesis topic to specifically involve North African Jewish Communities, including those from Morocco, Algeria, Tunisia and Libya. Also, her supervisor had retired from his position, and her new supervisor had insisted that adequate research into these regions required the ability to read French. Undaunted, she got an extension for her P.H.D. and she set about studying French. But in 1976, when my father died, she withdrew her application.

***

In 1982, at the age of 68, my mother decided once again to attempt her P.H.D. I remember her phoning me, and telling me with much amusement that she had received both her student card, and pensioner card, on the same day.

> I enrolled to do my P.H.D – I decided it's time to stop messing around with my life.

STUDY AS THERAPY

It turned out, however, that in order to complete the thesis she had started she was now also required to study Arabic as well as French, and she flatly refused to do this.

So she changed direction entirely, choosing to study for her P.H.D. a subject of great personal interest – the Holocaust. From a number of perspectives, this was a disastrous decision.

The new thesis was titled *'The Holocaust experience as mirrored in the literary testimony of K-Tzetnik 135633'*.

K-Tzetnik was a pseudonym for a renowned Jewish novelist, who was a survivor of the Holocaust. One of the highlights of my mother's life was meeting him in Israel, during the course of her research. But aside from this, her second-time P.H.D. experience was tumultuous.

To start with, researching was particularly difficult for her. The literature she was studying was gut-wrenchingly graphic. Instead of taking her out of her past, which had been her rationale for prior study, it drove her deeper into an introspective Holocaust experience at a personal and emotional level.

At an academic level, it was problematic as well. She had a relatively unsupportive supervisor who left her to her own devices until the work was almost ready for submission, and he then unexpectedly resigned, leaving her to complete her work virtually unsupervised. She was too emotionally invested and her thesis was too subjective. The examiners suggested she approach publishers to print the book for general readership rather than as a PHD thesis – *'the subjective approach makes the thesis interesting and stimulating reading but it fails to be a fully academic research paper'.*

Still, my mother chose to revise and re-submit her thesis – against the advice of the examiners.

Considerable revision was required by the Higher Degrees Committee, and in order to undertake this, she had to find a new supervisor. Eventually, a supervisor at the University of Cape Town – 1200 kilometres away – agreed to assist her. In 1987, fax machines and personal computers were in their infancy and the Internet did not yet exist, so remote connectivity involved support by letter or telephone. This was far from ideal, but she accepted the supervisor's offer, and reworked the thesis.

Among my mother's most precious possessions was a ticket in her name for her P.H.D. graduation ceremony for Tuesday 7 April 1987. This was issued by her university when the internal examiners approved her thesis, and agreed to confer the degree of P.H.D. on her. But before the graduation ceremony occurred, a report from the external examining committee (which in a cruel twist of fate was from a university in Germany) advised that – in the light of the subjective approach, and lack of adequate academic content – they could not support awarding the degree to her. The conferral of her P.H.D. degree never took place.

She must have been devastated.

But then, in her usual pragmatic style, she refused to accept defeat. She had done the work required, she had submitted the thesis, *her* university had accepted it, and that was that.

As far as she was concerned, she had a P.H.D. – even if she never had a certificate or graduation ceremony to prove it. And whenever she listed her academic achievements thereafter, her P.H.D. was always top of the list.

PART FIVE:
THE HOLOCAUST

I am eight years old. My sister and I sit in the reserved front row of the Yom HaShoah service – she is holding tightly onto my hand. My mother is not in her seat next to me – she is on the stage, addressing the hundreds of mourners around us, in Yiddish. I do not understand the words, but the raw emotion in her voice and the evocative language speak straight to my soul. The experience is harrowing.

NOT JUST A SURVIVOR

For as long as I can remember, the Holocaust loomed large in our lives. My mother justified her survival, and consequent determination to live, by a self-imposed obligation to share her experiences with everybody. This became the central force in her life. Her experiences defined her, they inspired her and gave substance to her every achievement. They were the signature tune of her life-song. And we, her children, absorbed this haunting melody through all our senses, into the core of our beings.

Her past – our heritage – was always, chillingly there.

From my earliest memory, my mother was involved with anything and everything to do with the Holocaust. She was a founder member of the Yad Vashem association in South Africa. She was on every committee and every board that educated about, or commemorated, the Holocaust. If there was a school function – no matter our involvement – and a Holocaust meeting on the same day, there was no discussion. My mother would be at the Holocaust function. It had front and centre stage in our lives. Always.

My whole life, I have religiously attended the annual Holocaust Memorial Service. In South Africa, it was an enormous commemoration that took place at West Park Cemetery, in Johannesburg, attended by thousands of people. I have a photo of me attending as a very young child, clearly showing my bewilderment at my mother's sadness. For many years, she was a key organiser of this function, and she usually gave the Yiddish speech – addressing the mourners who attended.

Now, as an adult in a different country, I still attend these services each year, although I have no need to be reminded of what happened. I carry the memory of this time in each of my cells, as clearly as if it were imprinted on my DNA. And I always find my mother's voice there, and the experience is always still harrowing.

My mother and Me at the Holocaust Memorial, Johannesburg, 1965

***

Throughout her life, my mother studied and taught about the Holocaust. Depending on her audience, the emphasis would differ. Usually, she spoke about her personal story – in much the same way as her personal story has been retold in this book: her early years in Lithuania, her family, the Ghetto, the concentration camps and briefly, her life after the camps.

But occasionally, when she was speaking to a more learned, informed or academic audience, she would bring in other elements – trying to explain the psychology of the survivor, the methodology of the Nazis, and the lessons that she felt should be taken from this dark period of history.

> My Curriculum Vitae describes milestones of my road – not from life to death, but from death to life. I may not have to live in the past, but the past continues to live in me.

As part of her story, I feel an obligation to pass on her beliefs, based around her answers to common questions she would receive at her lectures.

CHAPTER 19.
SURVIVAL

In a society where you have no rights, and your aggressor ceases to be governed by the laws of humanity, and the world stand by and fails to intervene, your chance of survival is minimal.

NOT JUST A SURVIVOR

My mother believed that survival depended on two things: chance and adaptability. And of these, chance was by far the most dominant factor – she felt it accounted for 85% to 90% of survival.

There were countless individual factors influencing chance: whether the guard walking past you that day was in a good or bad mood; whether the *Blitzwoman's* dog eating from the food trough ahead of you took too long, so you never got a chance to collect your meagre meal within the allocated half hour; whether you were lashed to death on trumped-up charges or were simply kicked into oblivion; whether you were too old, or too young, or too ill, or not ill enough, or you looked too Jewish, or looked not Jewish enough – all these, and every other random factor imaginable, influenced your chance of staying alive.

But amongst these many random factors, my mother spoke about one particular activity that greatly impacted on your chance of survival: the *selektion*.

In the beginning of the Nazi occupation, there was simply random shooting of Jews, often aided and abetted by the Lithuanians, in keeping with the objective of exterminating the Jewish people. But there was a war going on, and after a short while the Germans realised it was expedient to keep those Jews that were capable of working, alive. Those deemed still able to work – especially later in the course of the war – had a greater chance of being selected to remain alive. The *selektion* was thus the mechanism by which the Nazis surreptitiously weeded out all those residents of the Ghetto, or camp, that provided nothing to the Nazis by remaining alive. It was an activity that involved a clear agenda, but one that was hidden from the inmates.

Eventually, however, once the Jews began to suspect the true purpose of the *selektion*, they also realised there was, in some situations, a tiny way to influence that bias – by appearing strong; by appearing mentally alert; by appearing younger; by giving the impression that you were still useful. The first to be eliminated were thus the elderly, the sick and the children. Chillingly, even their death contributed to the Nazi war effort – their clothes, shoes, possessions, and even hair and skin and gold teeth implants, were used.

A *selektion* took place whenever there was a need to reduce the number of confined Jews – in the Ghettos, and in the concentration camps. All the Jews in that area had to present to the assembly point area and walk past the Nazi in charge. He usually pointed with a little stick – to the left, or to the right, and the person in the queue had to comply. There were police and guards and dogs to enforce his judgement. Sometimes individuals were selected, sometimes families. Initially, those being selected had no idea why, nor which side – left or right – was the better side. But over time they came to recognize that one side meant life, and the other meant death.

Selektions were not the only method used to remove large numbers of Jews from the Ghettos or camps. There were also regular requests for groups to volunteer for transfer – usually on the promise of better work and better conditions. In the beginning, people believed and volunteered. Over time, they learned not to trust, and volunteers were no longer voluntary, but coerced. In this way, people were moved around – usually transported to another location, sometimes for forced labour, more often, simply to be killed.

> For every *selektion* there was a different reason. At the beginning, they said it was just to make it more comfortable for the workers. Later on, they said they needed some workers in a very nice place so that the people would actually offer to go. If there were no volunteers, or not enough, then there was a selektion.

The Nazis had an additional motive for removing certain people from the Ghetto. They targeted all the educated and successful young people – the future leadership who might potentially have galvanised the others into some form of organised resistance.

> In 1942, all of a sudden, a demand came for 500 educated people with degrees, you know, the intelligentsia – as we called them – are needed to establish there some museum or libraries in the town itself, and that is a very good job. At that stage there was already hunger in the Ghetto, and hard work on the aerodrome from morning till night, so a lot of people volunteered.
>
> Not everybody could get amongst these 500 – it

SURVIVAL

was only the privileged ones – those that were in the *Judenraht*, their friends and sons and so on. All the best people from the Ghetto – the 500 elite men – volunteered, and we never saw them again. They were supposed to go in the morning and come back home at night, and then work the next day, but they never came back.

Eventually, after some time, we heard from the Lithuanians – from the peasants – that they were taken to the Ninth Fort and shot the same day.

***

The second factor that influenced survival was adaptability: what you did with that chance opportunity you received to survive another hour, another day, another week until the next *selektion*.

To survive, you had to became emotionally detached from normal life. When the people came to the camp, those that could accommodate, those that could become dehumanised, detached emotionally from the world where they were before, they could survive. The previous life was something to support them, to sustain them, it was something to think about, perhaps, and forget where you were, but you needed also to be detached from it. There were some people who could not bring themselves to get dehumanised in that way, to get acclimatised in the camp. Life in the camp was too much for them, then they just could not take it, and they gave up.

The longer you were in a camp, the more chance you had to survive because your personality changed, and you got more and more adapted to that sort of life. You became more like animals – striving for food and warmth. Nothing more. There was nothing that worried us anymore. We didn't worry about our families, because we knew our families are no more alive, and we were happy that they are not suffering.

In addition to this psychological adaptability, there were other factors that greatly influenced survival. Working conditions varied – some made it easier to survive than others. Working indoors, working in positions of authority, and working in the kitchens all facilitated survival. Some of this was luck – adding to the chance factor, and some, like in my mother's case, was a function of personality – her determination, her fearlessness, and her intelligence. Opportunities came her way – often due to her language skills, sometimes her astute reading of a situation, and often by her brutal honestly and willingness to take a calculated risk.

SURVIVAL

> These chances gave one a temporary break, even if not a lasting one. The chance of survival, once you had *not* been selected for extermination, relied mainly upon the person – by his or her behaviour and adaptation to the existing conditions. Some people were imbued with sustaining powers which life itself provides when all else is stripped away.
>
> Victor Frankel said: *The will to survive and the reason why, played a very important role in survival. If you have a why, then it doesn't matter how.* In our case the *why* was the hope to be reunited with our loved ones; to become part of a normal human society and lead a normal life again; and for revenge not to kill, but to see our torturers crushed. To see them punished for their crimes, and to experience the joy of seeing the Germans defeated. We knew that it had to come, but we did not know that we would live to see it.

Although my mother talked of doing almost anything to survive, she also made one thing abundantly clear: she would never, ever have benefited personally at the expense of another inmate. Quite the contrary. As part of her survival strategy, she helped others. In a situation where everyone had so little, she still shared – out of humanity and an inbuilt sense of what was right. And as much as she gave to others, so she received from them. Her friends went out on a limb for her, and she survived as a consequence. They in turn survived because she set things in place for them. When she talked of doing anything in order to survive, it was always in the context of her basic, unwavering morality.

It didn't matter how one survived, what the circumstances were. If you needed to eat dirt; if you had to live in filth; if you had to clean excrement with your bare hands; if you had to remove a mouse from your soup – nothing mattered. Except for the moral point of view.

> If people were strong enough morally, they would not choose to survive in the place of another. With my survival, I must not cause the death, or the suffering of another one. But some people decided that they can survive no matter the cost to another – those were the *Kappos*.

The *Kappos* – Jews who acted as police and henchmen, carrying out the work of the SS – survived, and benefited, at the expense of the other inmates of the concentration camps. General opinion of them was scathing. My mother considered them evil, but conceded that the circumstances of the time created survival behaviours that are difficult to judge in a normal world.

> They were the dregs of humanity – social misfits of normal society, denuded of all human feeling, possessing the qualities needed to do the dirty work of the SS.

They had a better life in the camp than outside of it by all sorts of dishonest means. They had cigarettes, drinks, the best of food and women. Their newly acquired power and rule over people that they could never have matched under normal circumstances, intoxicated them and they became inhuman. In many instances, worse than the Nazis.

They also did not go unpunished – they were either killed by their bosses or by inmates they had wronged. I say that history must judge them. We cannot judge them, because in that day and in that time, their state of mind, and those circumstances and in that environment, their sudden decisions to do what they did, cannot be analysed now, sitting in a peaceful, quiet society with a very clear mind, because all of our minds at that stage were not clear.

CHAPTER 20.
HOW COULD IT HAPPEN?

The Nazis, at Hitler's bidding, had as their main objective the extermination of the Jewish people, and they developed a detailed plan of how to do this.

The first step was to uproot the Jews from their homes and communities and incarcerate them in Ghettos. Once imprisoned in this way, the Nazis and their accomplices could take total control of every aspect of the Jews' lives – physical, emotional and social. The Ghetto inmates were totally at the mercy of their captors who dictated the terms by which one could remain alive – the possibility to work and the right to eat.

In each Ghetto a *Judenraht* was established – a council of Jewish 'leaders' whose task, on the pretext of serving the community, was actually to carry out Nazi orders – to ensure the exact and prompt implementation of directives issued by the Gestapo. When the Germans demanded a list of men for forced labour, the *Judenraht* provided it. When there was an order for a *selektion*, the *Judenraht* transmitted it.

> When they made the *Judenraht* we thought that the *Judenraht* was going to help us, you know, to find housing and to find work, and see that we get some food and all that. The Germans had it differently in their mind. They wanted the *Judenraht* to be the central address where they can come and demand and be obeyed.

But the Ghetto was just the first step in the Nazi's planned annihilation of the Jews. The second step, for those that survived, was to send them to concentration camps where the process of dehumanisation had been perfected. Whatever could be done to maximise the degradation of the human being, was done. They took away their children. They took away their clothes, their possessions, their hair, their names. They took away their dignity. They left them with nothing but the core of their beings and a number. And it continued for every moment and in every aspect of their existence, throughout their incarceration in the concentration camps.

> They kept telling us that we are vermin, we are worth being treated like vermin, we are nothing. When we were in a camp and food was distributed, this was in a big trough. There was 'soup'– whatever there was – warm water and some leaves and sometimes a bone or something. The dog was brought first, to choose from

the trough, if there was a bone or something that he liked it, and we had to watch it. And after the dog was satisfied, then we could get our portion of whatever it was. Just to show it to us, and it was always pointed out to us, always we felt it, that we are just nothing. We are not human.

The dehumanisation process had two effects. Firstly, it served to make the inmates feel worthless, to remove their identity, their individuality and their humanity. At the same time, the dehumanisation made it easy for the Nazis and the German population in general, to treat the Jews as non-humans, in turn enabling them to carry out unspeakable cruelty and unprecedented behaviour without any emotional repercussions.

The second aim they were having in the concentration camps was to teach their SS recruits, the upcoming leaders and guards, to teach them how to be cruel. So when they were brought to the camp, the young ones were taught and shown by the older ones, how easily inmates become dehumanised. Imagine what we looked like – very thin and being just in that one dress, and we were shaved of our hair, there was no face to us, nothing to identify as a woman, or even a human – it was nothing for them to look at us as little, I don't know, some animals.

So little by little they got to treat us and look at us and appreciate us as non-humans. They were applauded for their cruelty, admired for their ability to kill us – it's nothing – whatever they will do to us, there is no pain attached to it. Our blood is not blood. So it was, sort of, it was a training school for the SS men that had to be guards in the camp and the SS women as well. They were just as vicious, just as brutal and as bad as the men.

How could a woman be like that, be so vicious? And then she'd go home and very tenderly treat her children and her family, or her husband or her parents or whoever. How can this happen? But it happened.

One other purpose of the concentration camps was to keep the local non-Jewish population on side. Often, this was not hard – most of the locals were as passionately anti-Semitic as the Nazis – but where that was not the case, local compliance was achieved, both by propaganda and by fear.

The concentration camps were in the midst of – surrounded by – the civil population to teach them a lesson. They saw what was going on in the camps, how we were punished. They used to stand around and watch how 25 cuts were administered to us for any small, imagined transgression – 25 cuts that one never recovered from; or when a vicious camp leader was throwing a young woman or a young boy onto the electric fences and they were electrocuted. They were watching it all. And this was to inculcate in them fear, to warn them that the ones that don't listen, or the ones that rebel, that is what they are going to get. And the population was really very, very frightened. They, too, were terrorised.

CHAPTER 21.
RESISTANCE

The common image that the public has, that during the Holocaust Jews went to their deaths 'like sheep to the slaughter' infuriated my mother. She worked her whole life to ensure that the true story be told – that the annihilation of the Jews was due not to a passive act of compliance by a weak people, but rather the result of the immense evil that human nature is capable of.

> So whatever in our history will be written, it should *not* be that the Jews went like sheep to the slaughter; that they had not resisted. This is a fallacy that has to be undone, that has to be eradicated. Now when we come to talk about heroism, when we talk about heroism and courage and the rest of it, I want to emphasize that every hour of our life, to live an extra hour under those circumstances, this was courage, this was heroism. There is always active and passive, and we were denied the active. We couldn't do anything to our murderers, to our enemies, but at least we tried to defy them, by trying to want to live.

There were many reasons my mother gave for why most Jews did not actively fight back. Firstly – they were psychologically stunned. They couldn't comprehend that their former friends, neighbours and colleagues could do this to them, or that the civilians around them had become, overnight and with no provocation, their captors. And, they were overpowered by numbers – an entire population had risen up against them.

> In Lithuania it was impossible, because the Lithuanians had it against us. Lithuania was occupied by Russia for one year and Lithuanians had it in their heads that we, the Jews, brought the Russians, we have given their country to the Russians. They believed the Germans would be their saviours, that they will give them back their country. So as soon as the Germans were established in Lithuania, the first day, the Lithuanians started to kill Jews. That was their revenge. We could not step out of the Ghetto – they were shooting us off the bridge, or catching us and bringing us over to Gestapo. But in Poland, in Warsaw, it was a different story. The Poles hated the Jews – they never loved us – but they hated the Germans even more. So rebellion, aided by the local population, was possible.

Another major factor as to why they did not actively resist, was that in the Ghetto, the Jewish population didn't know the truth of what they were being told – particularly early on. When they were offered work elsewhere, or a chance at a better life, they took it. They jumped at the opportunity to work in supposedly better locations, and they believed the promises that they would be able to provide more comfort for their families. And the Nazis used these pretexts to entice them, and murder them.

> They used to come to a camp and say we want 20, 25 people to take you to establish a new camp. It was a draw-card, because in a new camp you can always get sort of a better work: you need workers in the barracks, you need workers in the camp, you need people to work in the kitchen. But in the old camps, you come and you find people there already, so all the good jobs are already taken. Even the worst job in the camp was better than to go for miles and work in the woods or the snow or work in a mine or anywhere on the roads or so on. So when they come and tell you that 20 people are being taken to a new camp, everybody wants to jump at the opportunity, everybody wants to go. But what do they do? They took the 20 people to the nearest wood and killed them. But we didn't know they were killing them. We found out after one of the lorries came back, written with blood on the side of the lorry in Russian, 'save yourself, don't listen to them, they are killing us in this and this way'. So then the people started to know. But before this, we didn't know.

But, perhaps the most compelling reason why there was no widespread Jewish resistance, was the simple drive to protect loved ones: the action of an individual carried brutal punishment for his whole family and his whole community.

Family ties in normal life are always strong, but in the camps, where people had nothing, they were even stronger. The Germans knew about it. They had very good psychologists working out every point in their program. Now, for every one that did something in a family, say he sabotaged or disobeyed or some little transgression, they punished the whole family. If they had somebody on the list and they came to look for him and he was not there, a young man, or a young woman or whatever, they would take away the whole family, and the whole neighbourhood – 40, 50, 60 – as hostages.

So if somebody amongst a group of people escaped, or were taken out of the Ghetto, or somebody would shoot or hurt a German, they would take these hostages and kill them in cold blood in the sight of all the others. They would bring the others to watch it. This is the punishment that you get for not listening or disobeying or whatever.

So this prevented we young people from leaving the Ghetto, and escaping into the woods. This knowledge prevented a lot of people that could really have saved themselves. The punishment that would come for saving my life, would be the lives of some other 50 or 60 or 80 or whatever. So I cannot do it. And that consideration of others, prevented a lot of rebellion.

It was only after a couple of years, when it was already realised by the Ghetto or the camp people, that nothing will help you in any case – you are doomed to die, your sentence is death – that's when they were really either rebelling, or trying to escape.

CHAPTER 22.
HER MISSION

My mother at the Yad Vashem Meeting

I think that my survival has something to do with a mission that I have, to perpetuate the memory of the Holocaust, to perpetuate the memory of six million Jews that were innocently murdered – cut down in the middle of their lives.

NOT JUST A SURVIVOR

To perpetuate the memory of the Holocaust was, for my mother, not a trite expression, nor an abstract concept, but a real, tangible motive in her life. Her educational background had taught her that people don't remember what they don't experience. They don't relate to, or learn from, what they don't understand. So her mission was to challenge and remove all these impediments to the memory of the Holocaust.

Through her words and her energy and her insights, she *made* people experience, understand and relate to the personal impact of what the Holocaust was to her as an individual, and not just dismiss it as a devastating occurrence in history. In this way, their experience of her story could be extrapolated to the stories of millions of others, and the enormity of the Holocaust could be truly absorbed, remembered and perpetuated.

> We the survivors are here for a short while only. Many of us have already passed, and we feel that only we, who have experienced all the horrors, all the depravity and barbarism of the inhumanity of the twentieth century, are capable of bringing it to you as living testimony. Only we can impress it on you – that it was so, it is true – in spite of all the attempts that comes from other quarters trying to deny it, to falsify our history. We are determined not to let our history be adulterated. We want it to be recorded as it was, and as it happened, in spite of pain that this may cause to some generations

or to some people or to some families that they have been involved in all this cruelty. I feel it is the duty of the coming generations to listen to it, to learn the lesson of it, and know it, in order that you should be able to pass it on to your children, and to future generations.

PART SIX:
ZIONISM, JUDAISM AND DEATH

CHAPTER 23.
ZIONISM

My greatest wish, if it is in any way possible, is to be buried in Israel.

NOT JUST A SURVIVOR

Long before the Holocaust galvanized the need for the existence of a Jewish Homeland, and long before the fledgling country became an independent State, my mother wanted to move there. Over the course of her life, in many different circumstances, she always wanted to live in Israel.

My mother had started investigating the option of migrating to Israel long before she even met Mokka, in a time when the modern national state not exist, other than as an ideological concept.

> In my third year at university, I have decided I wanted to go to Israel. There were some different ways. A friend of mine, who was a boyfriend of mine, was going there, so we have decided that he is going, perhaps I can go with him. But this didn't work out. I tried a different way.
>
> My grandfather lived in South Africa and he was a friend of Rabbi Cook who was in Israel, so he could have gotten for me a certificate to come to study there. But the subjects we studied in first year in Lithuania, they studied in third year in Israel. This meant I could go to Israel only as a first-year student and lose two years, so my father wouldn't let me go. He said, 'Just qualify here, and then you can go afterwards'. But times changed, and it also never happened.

Later, when she was married to Mokka, and it became evident that conditions for the Jews were becoming difficult in Lithuania, they started trying to secure papers to leave.

> My husband applied for papers. He had cousins in the States, in California, and he had applied to go to California. They had accepted us. His cousins didn't have children, they adopted my son, and sent us papers – but the Russians were already in Kovno, when our papers came, and they sent away our papers to Moscow, and we couldn't get them. My husband probably could have gone to Russia if I had wanted to go, but I wanted to go to Israel. He said to me, 'let's go to Russia', and I said 'no, I would rather wait and go to Israel.' And then the Germans occupied Kovno.

At the time of her liberation, a Jewish Brigade was formed to assist Jewish survivors to illegally migrate to Israel. People from that Brigade came to Bergen-Belsen, and my mother and some of her friends registered with them to go to Israel. In the meanwhile, for about two weeks, she travelled in Europe with a group of survivors, where they were all trying to make contact with their families. When she returned to Bergen-Belsen, by then no longer a concentration camp but a displaced persons camp run by the Allies, options started to open for her future. She had offers to migrate to Israel, South Africa or the United States. She was in poor health, and, uncharacteristically, she couldn't make a decision.

> Now I just couldn't decide where to go. I had three places where I had to choose, but I can't decide. So one evening I brought all my papers to a meeting with these soldiers (from the Israeli Jewish Brigade), with this whole group and I said to them, you decide for me where I should go. Here are all my papers, here is my state – as you see me – and I can't decide. They all decided – all of them – that I must go to South Africa, to my brother.

So once again, her decision to migrate to Israel was put aside.

Although she never migrated to Israel, my mother never lost her passion for the country. She loved Israel with an ideological fervour and visited many times, often for long stays. She went to study there, and attended courses at Yad Vashem.

When my sister got married in Israel, and my mother's first grandson was born there, she had even greater motivation to move there – but then my sister and her family returned to live in South Africa, so my mother shelved any further ideas of making *Aliyah* (the immigration of Jews from the diaspora to Israel) .

I often wonder how different her life would have been if she *had* migrated there from Lithuania. Of course, the whole chapter of her second family would never have been written, but I think, with her personality and her Zionist ideology, she would almost certainly have made a life in Israeli government. My mother followed Israeli politics, and was knowledgeable and vocal. She took Israel's fate almost personally – world decisions, for her, had only one filter – 'Is it good for Israel, or not'.

I remember the day Yitzhak Rabin, The Prime Minister of Israel, was shot. My mother was visiting us in Brisbane, and was sitting on the steps of the swimming pool, listening to the news. It was as if she had been personally punched in the chest – she bent over double and wailed – crying inconsolably, as if a family member had died. She was adamant that, after his death, peace would never come to Israel.

Years later, a few days before my mother died, she had a 'vision'. In her dream, Eli Wiesel had appeared to her.

> He sat on the end of my hospital bed, and we talked. It was wonderful. It was comforting. He told me everything would be alright. Everything would be alright for me. And everything would be alright for Israel. He told me not to be afraid – that peace will come to Israel.

The fate of Israel – even in the face of my mother's eminent death – carried as much weight, and was of equal significance to her, as her own.

CHAPTER 24.
JUDAISM

The Rabbi, at the consecration of my mother's tombstone, is making a speech. He addresses my sister and me, and the other mourners present.

'I know where Lea is', he says, with a confident smile. 'She is sitting in Heaven, close to God. And I am sure she is asking him very many difficult questions. I hope he is able to answer her to her satisfaction – because during the many hours she asked them of me, I never could.'

For the entire duration of her life, my mother was an observant Jew. Other than in the concentration camps, where she consumed anything that could be considered edible, she never, ever, ate anything that wasn't kosher. But, as concession to her pragmatism, outside of her home she was flexible and adaptable, eating fish or vegetarian cuisine that might not have been prepared under kosher conditions, but that nevertheless, was not categorically un-kosher.

Of necessity, both my parents worked in The Shop past the onset of the Sabbath on a Friday evening, and on Saturday mornings, but outside of this, my mother would never do 'work' such as writing, or sewing, on the Sabbath, and she attended synagogue on major Jewish Holidays. We always had traditional Friday night dinner, with candles and challah and prayers, and as teenagers, we were expected not to go out on a Friday night.

After she retired, my mother became even more observant. She attended synagogue services almost weekly, she observed the laws of Shabbat more diligently and she regularly attended Jewish religious groups and discussions.

Yet, despite all this, until a few weeks before her death, she was adamant that she did not believe in God. It was incomprehensible to her that a God could allow the Holocaust atrocities to occur, and the only conclusion she could come to was, therefore, that he did not exist.

When I challenged her on this paradox – her adherence to Jewish law but her non-belief in a God, she explained to me that Judaism, to her, was not about God. It was a culture, a tradition and an identity. Her observance was a way to respect the memory of her parents, and to perpetuate the traditions that they had believed in.

> Can you sleep without sheets? Of course not. To me, keeping Kosher is like sleeping with sheets – it is what I have always done, it is what is expected and it makes me feel comfortable. It is how I feel normal.

She also explained that adherence to Judaism was her ultimate act of defiance to the perpetrators of the Holocaust.

> If it was reason enough to be killed for, it is certainly reason enough to live by.

But, as with every aspect in her life, she sought validation of her ideas via study. Among her friends, over the years, were many learned rabbis – my husband often joked about the sanctity of our own marriage, since there were at least five rabbis present at our wedding. And, although she was always respectful of her rabbinic friends, my mother also argued and challenged them at every opportunity – ideologically and academically. She regularly attended religious classes, where she questioned anyone who was happy to debate with her – the Rabbis, the teachers, and her fellow students.

Two weeks before she died, when she was in hospital in Brisbane, her Rabbi flew up from Sydney for the day – simply to spend time with her. He was there as her friend rather than in any spiritual capacity, but he nevertheless related to me later, that at that visit my mother had told him she had reconciled her relationship with God. Sometime during the process of her illness, she had finally made peace with her God and was happy at the concept of being reconnected with her long-deceased loved ones.

Having accepted that there was, in fact, an afterlife, in a moment of lucidity, she contemplated the practicalities involved – wondering out loud whether her two husbands would be jealous of each other, and how she would divide her time between them – and more importantly:

> How will Michael recognise me? He was only a baby when he died, and now I am an old woman.

And then, in her usual pragmatic way, she decided that – if it really was Heaven where she was going to meet up with them – the problems would have all been resolved in advance, and she really needn't worry about these things at all.

CHAPTER 25.
DEATH

(AUSTRALIA, 2000)

Finally the monster has a name.

After weeks of lurking around, posing as a much-more-benign stroke, causing unexplained falls and progressively bizarre behaviour, it has been unmasked by an MRI scan.

It is a malignant Glioblastoma.

In July 2000, the day before her 86th birthday, my mother was diagnosed with a malignant brain tumour.

It was the worst day of my life.

We had been alerted to the fact that she was unwell by my daughter, Kerry, who was concerned that her behaviour was uncharacteristic. She had had a couple of falls while guiding student groups at the Sydney Jewish Museum, and she just wasn't herself.

We brought her to our home in Brisbane for her usual rest and recovery, but instead of recovering, things got progressively worse, until I couldn't leave her on her own for a moment. Desperately, I sought an urgent geriatric consultation, fearing that she had rapid onset dementia.

But it was worse.

From the time of first concern to the day of her death, was two short months – the longest two months I had ever endured. But in retrospect, the disease was kind. It took her quickly and with no pain. She didn't seem to suffer.

As it was, my mother never feared death. She had already lived her worst nightmare. By her reckoning, she should have died many times over in the concentration camps, together with her six million compatriots. So, in her own eyes, every day that she lived was a bonus.

To me, it was ironic that the final assault was to her brain. It had always been her pride and joy. There was no doubt in my mind that her unique, self-preserving yet selfless qualities as a human being were as much a tribute to her exceptional brain as to her indomitable spirit.

So it was such a bitter twist that this monster had infiltrated the exact core of her that had kept the other monsters in her life at bay, to wreak havoc in the temporal region of her brain.

It stripped her of her senses of taste and temperature. It stripped her of her independence, eventually keeping her bedridden and immobile. It stripped her of her personality, her assuredness, her independent spirit, and her intellect – replacing these with compulsive finger tapping and obsessive counting – as if concentrating on the next number could somehow stem the tide of relentless loss.

Quickly, but oh, so slowly, the disease consumed her – her sense of time, her sense of humour, her sense of self.

But her Holocaust experiences – the theme song of her life, never melodious but always hauntingly, powerfully present – somehow remained.

And then, finally, she was set free.

When I think of her today, the nightmare of that time has been replaced. The essence of her has returned, and the sadness has been transformed into awe and thankfulness for who she was, and always will be.

She will never, ever, be forgotten.

ADDENDUM:
REFLECTIONS ON BOBBA

During the writing of this book, whenever I told people who had known my mother about my intent to document her stories, everyone had their own story to offer.

Is the one about this in it? What about that one? You must include the one about her Scrabble words, or her spelling with a Yiddish accent, or her legendary bad driving. And so it went.

Many, many people wanted to add recollections of their special bond with her to the book – so here are a very small selection of 'reflections': from her grandchildren; from people who weren't her grandchildren but felt as if they were; and from her sons-in-law – only a few of the countless people whose hearts she touched.

EYTAN

My grandmother, Lea Leibowitz had a profound and lasting impact on my life. But as I have been thinking of her, one thing in particular has kept popping into my head: my grandmother was always fond of telling me stories.

She told me many beautiful stories from her happy life before the war. Stories of picking wild strawberries in the forest behind her family's log cabin, of skating on a frozen lake in the winter time, and of the indescribable joy she experienced in the moment when her son was born.

And she also told me many horrific stories from her life during the war. Stories of hunger and deprivation; stories of life in the concentration camps, and of the despair felt at the death of her five-year old son (after whom I am named), and almost all of her extended family at the hands of the Nazis. Stories that almost felt like fantasy to me, so unfathomable were the barbarism and suffering they spoke of.

But my favourite stories were always those that came next: the stories of rebirth, and rebuilding, and resurrection. For me it was these stories that defined my grandmother. These stories took all the brutality and hate and destruction she endured, and rather than allowing these experiences to destroy her soul, using them instead to find wonder in the world once more. To find love and forgiveness and hope in even the smallest, seemingly most insignificant of things.

My grandmother died twenty years ago. After living an incredible and full life, at the age of 86 she developed a brain tumour which took her within weeks. Mercifully it was quick and painless. Her last two weeks were spent in a hospital bed in Brisbane, drifting in and out of awareness; sometimes conscious of her surroundings, but mostly not.

I travelled to Brisbane in that time to visit with her; to say goodbye, really. It was heart-wrenching when my beloved grandmother looked at me and didn't even know who I was. It was devastating to see a strong, proud, indomitable woman, who had endured and survived so much, reduced to a semi-human state. Someone once told me that when God decides to destroy you, he goes for your mind first. But in that hospital, I really felt those words. I felt them as urgently as if they were being tattooed onto me, just like the numbered tattoo on the forearms of so many of those who survived the atrocity of the Shoah (Jewish holocaust).

I went to see my grandmother one morning in the hospital. Without warning she sat bolt-upright in her bed. Unlike every other time I had gone to see her on that final visit, this time she saw me, recognised me, and called me to come closer. I took a seat beside her and held her hand, and she started talking clearly and calmly. She wanted to tell me a story. It was a story she had told me many times before, but for some reason, this was the story she wanted to tell me again, that morning, in the hospital in Brisbane.

And the story she told me was this:

"*After the war, the refugee relocation people managed to locate my only surviving relative – my brother Hymie, who was living in South Africa. So they decided to send me there. There were no commercial planes back then, so along with maybe 500 Jewish survivors,*

I was put on ship in Lisbon, and sent off to my new life at the other side of the world.

It was a long journey – about four weeks. And about halfway through the journey, we stopped for three days in an African country – I can't remember which one – to take on supplies and fresh water.

None of us left the ship the whole time – after all those years under the Nazis, we were just too scared. So we had no interaction with the locals.

But on our second day, a young African boy came onto the ship. He was the first black person I had ever seen – remember I had lived my whole life until then in Lithuania and Poland and Germany, where everyone in those days was white as the winter snow. I remember thinking how healthy his skin looked compared to all the survivors on the ship.

He had come onto the ship to deliver a bunch of bananas – a huge bunch of bananas so big that in my memory it was bigger than him! And it was the first time I had ever seen a banana. These are tropical fruits and common today, but where I grew up they just didn't exist.

Actually, it was the first time any of the 500 people on that ship had ever seen a banana. And none of us knew what to do with them. I remember one man took a big bite of it, skin and all, and spat it out. And I remember my friend tried to cut it up with a knife and fork.

But then the young African boy showed us what to do: how to peel it and how to eat it. I took my first bite, and it was the most beautiful, delicious, exquisite thing I had ever tasted: a sweetness that I will never forget.

As she spoke, my grandmother laughed so hard at the memory of that banana and her friend trying to eat it with cutlery. Tears rolled down her cheeks, and her bright blue eyes twinkled in a way that only her eyes ever could. It was infectious, and I couldn't help myself. I found myself laughing and crying with her, too.

She died a week later. That was the last lucid conversation I remember having with my grandmother. It was like the extraordinary lady I had known all my life as "Bobba" (grandma in Yiddish) had cast off her illness for a brief moment, just to tell me that one last story. It is something I will never forget.

And ever since then, I have never been able to eat a banana without thinking of my grandmother, and of her boundless love and optimism, and feeling like I live in a world of endless goodness and endless possibility.

DAN

It's the early 80s and I'm in a car, hurtling down Berea Road en route to Park Lane Hospital in Johannesburg. I'm maybe seven years old, and thanks to a stupid prank by my best friends' older brother and a heavy oak front door, my right index finger is bloodied, mangled and throbbing with pain. A traumatic experience for any child you'd think, except oddly, all I can remember about the incident was my grandmother – she was, after all, the one at the wheel, racing me to the hospital in the middle of the day when no-one else could come to my rescue. Actually, I giggle when I think back to this moment, because through all the mayhem, bleeding and crying, she had somehow gotten it into her head that I had been 'playing with nails'. 'Vy vere you playing vith nails?!' 'No, Bobba', I kept insisting, 'I caught my finger*nail* in the door', to which the response was invariably 'but vy vere you playing vith nails'??!! This went on all the way to the hospital and I'm pretty sure the doctors who fixed my finger that afternoon, having been duly briefed by her, were all under the impression that I had been 'playing vith nails'.

Anyway, the point of the story is not my finger, nor my abundance of childhood bravery, but rather the lady I was lucky enough to call my 'Bobba'. As per the anecdote, she was always there for her family, and I'd like to think especially for us grandkids (and I'm sure my brothers and cousins will agree). Through our childhoods, she was a permanent fixture. At our homes, her apartment, holidays, birthdays, excursions, shabbats, *chagim*, *simchas* – you name it, she was there and involved, doting on us kids as only a loving and devoted Bobba could. I have never claimed to have been her favourite – that title is hotly contested between my older brother and younger cousin, but I know my Bobba loved me with all her heart, as she did all her grand-kids, and that was plenty for me.

When we all moved to Australia the roles changed somewhat. She was still as loving and doting as ever, but was aging and not able to keep up as she once did. So, we, the grandkids, started looking out for her. For my part, I pledged to keep her entertained. I was a goofy teenager and not afraid to make a fool out of myself in front of family and friends. It was not uncommon for 'performances' to unfold at our place or hers, usually following a Friday night Shabbat dinner. One time I was doing an impromptu comedy routine that called for me to eat bread. My Bobba, not wanting to keep the audience waiting rushed to the kitchen to fetch some, but apparently forgot that I needed to EAT it as part of the act, and presented a frozen slice of rye. My reaction to that, and then hers prompted a roar of laughter from the crowd and all was dutifully captured on home VCR by my uncle (who holds a large cache of incriminating video-evidence against me, btw). Yep, regardless of personal embarrassment, it was my job to make Bobba laugh. Even during her final days, I would get up to all kinds of shenanigans in her hospice room, just to get her to smile, including an all-out tap recital to blues music (don't ask – I was studying a tap requirement at drama school, my brother was at music college – do the math). I was also given the (unofficial) role of 'designated driver' when I turned 18 and got my driver's license. I would give my Bobba rides home most Friday nights and whilst it was only a quick 20-minute drive, over the years and countless trips we somehow managed to chat and laugh about everything – topics ranging from girls, to money, to matzah. Often, she would tap me on the leg with a warm kind smile – 'Don't vorry Dunkas" she would say using an old childhood nickname reserved for family members only, "everything vill vork out for you'. These were very special one-on-one moments with her and I'll never forget them (and you know what, she was right – things did work out for me in the end).

It's now been many years since she passed, and not surprisingly she continues to be an inspiration to me and anyone who knew her. Not just because she was incredibly intelligent (she held five degrees and spoke at least eight languages). Not just because she was so headstrong and determined. Not because of her endless devotion to Jewish life and its importance to the rest of us. And not because she was the undisputed matriarch of our family. For me, it was because of her capacity to love. As an adult, and one with kids, I stand in absolute awe at what my grandmother went through and how she was able to persist and above all, continue to love. Here is a person that lost just about everything – most of her family and friends perished in the Holocaust, along with her then-husband and 4-year-old son Michael, who was literally taken from her arms. She survived this and the horrors of the Holocaust and the concentration camps, and then somehow found the strength, determination and love to reconstruct her life, re-marry, have more children and then grandchildren. HOW?!! How was she able to do this? I don't think I would have the strength or the heart under the same circumstances, honestly. But that was my Bobba – one truly remarkable lady. And one that I miss very much.

Bobba, I hope you are happy and content where-ever you are. I hope Mum is with you and the two of you are smiling. I hope you'll be waiting for me when I get up there. I hope I'll get a chance to make you laugh again. I miss you. All my love, Dunkas.

YANIV

I don't remember a lot about my grandma.

I was pretty young and I'm aware when she was around.

We would go to her place most weeks for Friday night dinner and she always had the table set and maybe a guest or two.

I used to love the chopped liver and challahs, and she used to make chicken feet soup which was surprisingly good.

I remember her eyes more than anything. She had piercing blue eyes and when I think of her that's what comes to me to this day.

I remember her singing along to McDonald's adverts and humming the tune to McChicken - it seemed to make her happy.

She taught me how to play Rummicub and we used to play that a lot.

My memory of her is tied up with my mom and dad, in the Friday night dinners, and sometimes everyone would just get into these laughter fits that seemed to last forever.

My brother Dan moved into her apartment after she passed away and re-did it. At that stage, I spent a lot of time in that apartment and I remember having moments of growing up there, of becoming more aware. It's not so much a memory of Bobba but something about the place still carried her presence and I always associate those times with her ....

I wasn't there when she passed away. I was in Israel and I spoke quite a bit with my folks at the time but death really didn't mean what it does to me now.

I have no negative memories of her.

Every year she gave me a card on my birthday and every year she wished me the same – success with my songs and with my health and I kept those cards a long time. It was only this year, when my mother passed away and when I started to really work through the process of letting go that I decided it would be therapeutic to chuck them out and let go.

I remember Eytan being much closer with her and sitting with her.

I just have fond feelings of her and an intuition that she was a great person. Her essence and spirit are entwined in my mother and my family and all the memories I carry of her and them and that means a lot to me.

It's a weird thing being that young and just not really knowing, but my soul definitely recognizes that there was a connection.

I'm sure there was a lot more to our relationship and probably many little things that happened, but it's all just sort of bundled up in her blue eyes and in my mom... like everything has bled into everything and just feels like love.

DAVID

Just Bobba.

To other people, Bobba was an unstoppable force – the kind that actually moves immovable objects. To me, she was just Bobba – not like anyone else's grandmother, not like my other grandmother. Just Bobba. When other kids were talking about their Bobba, it didn't really feel right – as if someone else had borrowed her – because she defined the label, rather than it being a label given to her.

My memories of her are somewhat distant – she was far away from wherever I was: Johannesburg, Sydney and occasionally trips to Israel. But when she would arrive regularly, she would stay with us for extended periods, a month or two at a time. Her visits would always bring two constants to every day.

Firstly, the exercise bike would be dragged out and oiled for her to ride. She swayed side to side and peddled for what seemed an eternity but would probably have been a single episode's worth of Bold & the Beautiful. If she hadn't used the bike during the day, then she would go for a swim in the pool that only she and my dad used, even if the rain had lightly started.

The second constant was the food – specifically *taiglach*, which are syrupy hard biscuits of goodness designed to extract dental fillings. Baking and cooking were such strongly defined aspects of her in my memory – I still think of the time spent next to her in her little kitchen in Sydney making *latkes* almost as fast as I could eat them. To this day, the word Bobba is synonymous with *latkes* and I will order them wherever I can find them. I was always encouraged to eat and probably got my love of food from the large helpings that accompanied the times we gathered to eat a roast dinner on Friday nights.

One of her biggest gifts was a love of family. I know the story of her discovering that two brothers, who lived in the same town and were both Holocaust survivors, had stopped speaking to each other. For her this was incredulous, as family is family and never to be torn apart. So she made up her mind to sit the two down and get them to see eye-to-eye. Whether or not this ever eventuated I do not know but I do understand the enormity of the importance of family.

Her other gift, a lot more tangible to me, was the start of my high school education. She made sure I could afford to go to school in the first year we moved to Brisbane. That first year's history assignment was actually a family history, which I based on her, which gave me a very academic insight into her life (as much as a thirteen-year-old could grasp). I did not realise at the time what a rarity it was that a young woman could attend University in the 1930s (in Eastern Europe and Jewish no less). I remember in my later school years explaining to her that the chemistry and physics I was learning 60 years later was literally rewriting the atomic principles she had studied in University.

A lot of our discussions were quiet, me listening, her talking – but in a somewhat impersonal way – a recollection of the past with stories of a different person enduring such horrors – not the beautiful, leathered face with blue eyes and a smile that sat before me. There was always that thin smile, a glint, a spark behind that face that sometimes erupted into uncontrollable laughter when something appealed to her sense of humour (usually at Friday night dinners with her whole family together).

The other remarkable skill that stood out was language – I struggled to barely learn and then forget four different languages. She was conversant in at least four and had a grasp of another five. I remember her putting down the phone after talking to her friends in Yiddish and continuing to speak it to us for at least ten seconds before swapping back to English after the blank stares she received (every time). I still wonder to this day what language she dreamed in?

The hardest part for me was to watch this incredibly intelligent, independent and capable person unravel as her sickness took hold. She very quickly became a little old lady who struggled to do the simplest of tasks, and could not have possibly been Bobba. It simply wasn't fair.

My Bobba was a presence – someone who took over when she entered a room. Someone who always had a light in her smile. Someone who still lives on in the stories she told, the stories told of her and the food that I love.

KERRY

I was Bobba's favourite. Although I'm sure if you asked her other four grandchildren, they'd all say they were her favourites. But I was the youngest and also the only girl – so I really believed I was the favourite.

I was only 18 when she died. With the exception of the last year of her life, I never lived in the same city as her. I don't have many tangible memories, and yet to this day my Bobba is without a doubt the most influential person in my life. I was fortunate enough to both inherit some of her genes and absorb her core values and essence through her stories.

I loved spending time with Bobba. From a very young age we would spend many late-night hours talking. We talked mostly of her childhood, her family and the Holocaust. For as long as I could remember I knew that my Bobba was 'A Survivor'. I knew that the man in the picture was her husband who was killed and that the boy in the photo was Michael – her baby.

In hindsight I don't recall any specific details of our talks, or even if I did any of the talking. I do know however that through her stories her values, determination, spirit, intelligence and her very essence were evident.

I do have some seemingly random memories of Bobba

– almost snapshots that come to me in the strangest of circumstances:

- Walking past a thrift store and seeing costume jewellery on display will bring back memories of me, as a young girl, trying on her extravagant 'good' jewellery. It was mostly broken costume jewellery, but it was always in bright colourful matching sets, that were often coordinated with her outfits.

- Sitting at the Community Swimming Pool watching my infant swim in one lane while older men and women with their swim caps and nose plugs swim in the next lane, reminds me how much my Bobba loved to swim! She regularly swam laps back and forth for hours in our swimming pool, or sometimes swam laps in the ocean at Bondi Beach – quite literally swimming the length of the beach parallel to the shore.

- Seeing groups of Jewish ladies at our local JCC, gathered around small tables playing cards, always reminds me of the competitive card and Rummicub games that Bobba enjoyed. It was always a treat when she visited as I was allowed to stay up late and play Rummicub. I certainly attribute some of my competitive nature to those fiery games at night.

- Teaching my daughter how to plait Challah brings back memories of the Challah that Bobba made every Friday night – and in fact memories of all the different foods she used to make. She always had food around and insisted on preparing me a little something to eat every time I entered her apartment - irrespective of whether I was hungry or not.

I do remember that feeling of sitting in Shul with her on Shabbat and Holidays and how, many years after she had gone, looking over to the seat that she always sat in and expecting to see her there.

I do remember how proud of my involvement in Zionist youth movements she was, as well as how proud she was of my academic success.

I do remember that she never yelled at me and that the only time she ever yelled; it was so out of character that I immediately called my parents in tears to tell them something was wrong with her. That 'something' was the first symptom of the brain tumour that would quickly take her life.

And I do remember her obsession with daily 'Soapies' – something that seemed rather incongruous with her sensible, intelligent side. She never could miss an episode of *The Bold and the Beautiful* – and consequently no-one could visit or call from 4.30-5.00 every weekday. If they did, and they were lucky, she would let them in without a word and make them wait until the show was over. I too began to take an interest in *The Bold and the Beautiful*.

Every week, if I didn't have classes or was feeling homesick, I went over at 4.30 to watch the show with her. Never a word was spoken, until it was over or during a rare ad break. After, we dissected every second of the show and characters in great detail. I could tell you more about Ridge and Thorne Forester and Stephanie and Eric, than any of Bobba's real friends. I'm sure the characters would have benefited, as I often did, from her super pragmatic, no-nonsense, non-holding back advice. In hospital, when she was dying, I carried on updating her to the very end about the characters' lives, speaking to her as if they were real people (in much the same way she talked and thought about them). I'm sure the nursing staff thought we mixed in very interesting circles.

I know that my sense of Jewish identity, Jewish culture, Zionism, fierce determination to persevere, to fight for what is right and just, is owed in part to her. Whether through the genes that I inherited from her or by osmosis from her stories, the impact she has had on who I have become, is immeasurable.

I sometimes wonder what she would think about the world today:

- My Shul in America for instance – so warm and inclusive to everyone, and yet reform – the antithesis of her observant orthodox practices.

- Politics. Would she support a president who was supportive of Israel but divisive and spreading racial hatred to all other minority groups?

- And what would she think of my daughters – two blonde-haired, blue-eyed, strong-willed Americans – one named after her and one named after her son Michael.

KERRY

There was a time when I couldn't imagine that the important people in my life (my husband and children) would never know this incredible woman that was my Bobba. A photo of her in pride of place in my living room and being able to tell my daughters who they were named after, plays a small part in helping keep her memory and her stories alive. Passing on her legacy is so important to me.

STACEY

Bobba. A Yiddish term used to describe a grandmother.

Although not biologically my grandmother, Bobba treated me as if I was her grandchild and I looked to her for the same guidance and love I looked to from my own grandparents.

I know my siblings, Melissa and Trevor felt the same way.

It is through a unique and special bond with Bobba that my siblings and I learnt not only important life lessons but were able to experience Jewish traditions, some of which were unfamiliar to us, but unique to Bobba as a result of her life.

She was in all meanings of the word, our Bobba too and we are all grateful to our cousins for sharing her with us.

Bobba's stories and values were imparted to us as children during our visits to her home whilst she 'force fed' us potato *latkes*, always insisting we needed to eat more and ensuring that we didn't leave without our takeaway food. A tradition which continues in all of our households after each and every family meal.

In my later teenage years and adult life, I have found myself interacting with more non-Jewish people. Whenever someone asks me about my Jewish traditions or about my knowledge of the Holocaust, my instinctual response is to share stories told to me by Bobba or my memories of her. My identity as a Jewish person is directly linked to my memories of Bobba.

Strong, determined, generous and loving are the words I would use to describe her. My relationship with Bobba has had a valuable impact on shaping the person I am today, and I am constantly reminded of her influence in my life

When Bobba passed away in 2000 I was 14 years old. I remember feeling a deep sense of heartbreak, mourning her passing alongside the entire family. Bobba was a special member of our family.

Each time my siblings and I visit the Jewish Cemetery at Macquarie Park we visit Bobba. We each take the time to carefully select a stone to place on Bobba's grave, stand together for a few moments and remind each other of our favourite memories of, and times with, Bobba. Our actions are a clear reflection of how much love we had and still feel for her.

With Bobba I always felt unconditional love and I know each member of my family felt the same.

YEHUDA

I always had a warm and wonderful relationship with my mother-in-law, based on love and mutual respect. This was a relationship separate to being married to her daughter.

Long before she became my mother-in-law, she showed me a remarkable kindness that expressed her belief in me as an individual.

I was a struggling student in Israel, studying at the Hebrew University. My parents were not in a position to help me, and I paid for my studies by working numerous part time jobs – labouring, tutoring – whatever I could get, in order to finance my studies.

I had been to visit Sheila – then my girlfriend – in South Africa, (sponsored by a company for whom I had worked) and had met her parents there. Bobba and I immediately found common ground.

During that visit we shared many interesting conversations and discussions – in Hebrew – around Israel, politics, economics and my studies – and then I returned to Israel to continue my studies there.

Imagine my surprise – and amazement – when a letter arrived at my home in Jerusalem some weeks later, from

Bobba, containing a cheque – a gift – to help me purchase books and aid my studies.

I don't remember if it was for $100 or $200 – but whatever it was, it was a lot of money at the time, and an incredible help to my situation. I was blown away that she had believed in my potential, and was so willing to help me – a relative stranger – fulfill my goals.

Many times, over the thirty years that she was my mother-in-law, we both joked about what a great investment she had made.

I never forgot the gift she had given me – more important than the money was the fact that she believed in me and cared enough to show it in a tangible way.

JONATHAN

Bobba used to joke that she loved her sons-in-law more than she loved her daughters. The relationship we had with her – it could have been true. And we, in turn, loved her back.

I have so many stories of her to recall, but the one that stands out most in my memory is this:

Bobba had bunions – partly due to the non-fitting clogs she was forced to wear during her years in the concentration camps. They bugged her – and she always talked of getting them fixed. But she had other medical issues, and was considered a risk for elective surgery, so we discouraged her.

Eventually, after years of nagging – *At least, if I die on the operating table, I'll go to heaven with straight feet!* – I arranged for a colleague to do bunion corrections on both feet. It was a time when everyone was leaving South Africa, and he did the surgery the day before he emigrated – leaving me responsible for the post-op care.

Everything went well, and she had wires through two toes on each foot, and plaster casts, for six weeks. She crocheted blue covers for her casts, and participated in normal life – even participating in a family day out boating (in an inflatable boat) on the river in Zululand.

Eventually the casts came off, and the healing looked good. Then came time to remove the wires – poking through the front of her toes. There were big discussions. Ideally, they should be removed under general anaesthetic – but we were trying to avoid this. Local anaesthetic was useless – the wires were in bone – too deep to be affected by local. We procrastinated, trying to find an optimal solution.

One day, when just she and I were at home alone, she approached me.

'Just take them out', she said. 'Now – while nobody here is around to stop you. I'll be fine – I'm tough – just do it!'

And so I did. No anaesthesia – nothing at all. It must have hurt incredibly – and I think it hurt me more than it hurt her. But she never uttered a word – just stoically lay there while I pulled these wires from her feet – like removing four large splinters embedded in bone.

Bobba and I were both still pale and sweating from the experience when my wife returned home a short time later. I looked at her guiltily, when she demanded to know what we had done – but Bobba had a broad, innocent grin on her face.

'Look', she said, pointing at her straight feet – 'they are beautiful. Thank you, Jon'.

It was a clear example of her steely determination to overcome obstacles by sheer endurance, when she made up her mind to.

I never forgot it.

ABOUT THE AUTHOR

Rochy Miller is the daughter of a Holocaust survivor – Lea Leibowitz. This memoir, her mother's story, has been a lifetime in the making.

Rochy is a retired medical doctor, who, like her mother, holds a swathe of other qualifications, and dabbles a little in each.

She has studied creative writing, and holds both Medical Journalism and Master of Journalism degrees. She has published numerous short stories and articles, as well as a series of Text Books in the field of Aesthetics Education.

Originally from South Africa, she now lives in Brisbane, Australia, with her husband – but spends much of her time travelling to Florida, USA, where her two young granddaughters live.

When not travelling, she can be found pursuing her other favourite creative pursuits: painting and toy-making, and – like her mother – baking up a storm in her kitchen.

www.ingramcontent.com/pod-product-compliance
Lightning Source LLC
Chambersburg PA
CBHW020418010526
44118CB00010B/309